MICHAEL GREEN

BAPTISM

ITS PURPOSE, PRACTICE & POWER

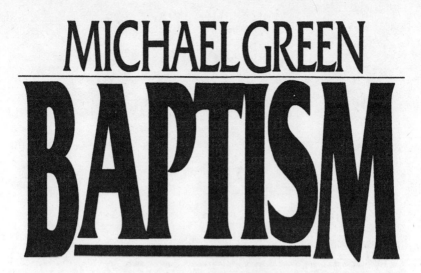

INTERVARSITY PRESS
DOWNERS GROVE, ILLINOIS 60515

Published in the United States of America by InterVarsity Press, Downers Grove, Illinois, with permission
from Hodder & Stoughton, London, England.

InterVarsity Press is the book-publishing division of InterVarsity Christian Fellowship, a student
movement active on campus at hundreds of universities, colleges and schools of nursing. For information
about local and regional activities, write Public Relations Dept., InterVarsity Christian Fellowship, 6400
Schroeder Rd., P.O. Box 7895, Madison, WI 53707-7895.

Cover illustration: Roberta Polfus

ISBN 0-8308-1713-1 (cloth)
ISBN 0-8308-1211-3 (paper)

Printed in the United States of America

Library of Congress Cataloging in Publication Data

Green, Michael, 1930-
    Baptism.

    1. Baptism.   2. Infant baptism.   3. Baptism in the
Holy Spirit.   I. Title.
BV811.2.G74   1987   234'.161   87-29876
ISBN 0-8308-1713-1
ISBN 0-8308-1211-3 (pbk.)

17	16	15	14	13	12	11	10	9	8	7	6	5	4	3	2	1
99	98	97	96	95	94	93	92	91	90	89	88	87				

In memory of my parents,

who brought me to baptism

PREFACE _____ 9

1 CONFUSION REIGNS! _____ 11

2 BACK TO THE BEGINNING _____ 21

3 THE BAPTISMS OF JOHN AND JESUS _____ 33

4 BAPTISM: WHAT DOES IT MEAN AND WHAT
  DOES IT DO? _____ 45

5 THE BAPTISM OF BELIEVERS—AND THEIR CHILDREN   59

6 OBJECTIONS CONSIDERED _____ 81

7 BAPTISM AND CONFIRMATION _____ 101

8 'REBAPTISM' _____ 113

9 BAPTISM IN THE HOLY SPIRIT _____ 127

PREFACE

Christian baptism is a thorny subject. It seems to be getting thornier all the time. There have always been baptised people who show no signs of spiritual life, and this provides an enormous problem for the church. In reaction, there are those, and their numbers are on the increase, who have turned their backs on baptism altogether, and regard it as an optional extra, provided you have new life in Christ. A great many people are very dissatisfied with infant baptism, and want to be rebaptised. Then there are those in some of the House Churches who will not accept you into membership unless you are rebaptised. Baptism and confirmation remain difficult areas. And there is a whole nest of confusion which has settled round that little phrase 'baptism in the Holy Spirit'.

I have written this little book because I knew of no other that examined, from an Evangelical Anglican perspective, this collection of issues. I have on my shelves no short and readable treatment which I could put in the hands of those who come trying to find their way through the maze, as they wrestle with problems like the meaning of baptism, confirmation, infant baptism, 'rebaptism' and baptism in the Holy Spirit. In preparing it, I want to acknowledge my indebtedness to the Grove booklets on baptism which flow from the pen of Bishop Colin Buchanan, a friend and erstwhile colleague at St John's Theological College, Nottingham. I also want to thank Sister Margaret Magdalen, friend and erstwhile colleague at St Aldate's Church, Oxford, now working in Botswana, for the help and insight she has afforded me by conversation and by correspondence. Needless to say, none of the errors and inadequacies of this little book must be laid at their door.

I know that in writing this book I am not merely laying my neck on the block but, if that were possible, half a dozen necks on the block! Because of the many vested interests in so sensitive an area as Christian baptism, I realise that I am bound to make more enemies than friends. So be it. I only tried to help! But two things are abundantly clear to me as I have attempted this book. One is that I have become increasingly aware of what a rich, complex and many-splendoured thing baptism is. The other is, how little I have plumbed its depths.

Thank God for the gospel!

And thank God for baptism, its sign and seal!

Michael Green
St Aldate's, Oxford, Christmas 1986

1
CONFUSION REIGNS!

Do you know that delightful negro spiritual, 'Denomination Blues'? It is, appropriately, sung by Muddy Waters. It runs through the different emphases of denomination after denomination, and it ends up 'You gotta have Jesus, and that's all'.

Yes, you gotta have Jesus: that is absolutely central. But unfortunately it isn't all. Once you 'have Jesus' you need to live for him, and be identified with his followers. In the early days of the church you found one clear and obvious body of people who followed Jesus. They were the Christian church. Just like that. No descriptive adjectives like 'Baptist Church' or 'Roman Catholic Church' or 'Orthodox Church'. Just church. One body of people. One large extended family, if you like. Of course they had all sorts of differences. If you joined in the worship of the early Jerusalem Church you would find all kinds of practices from Judaism continuing among the Messianic Jews who formed the Church. If you went to a large secular city like Antioch, you would find far less of that, and a community who did not fuss too much about how they used the sabbath or whether they circumcised their boys. There were lots of differences. Of course. How dull it would be if we were all the same. But there were certain central things which they all held in common. And one of them was baptism.

One baptism?

Listen to the apostle Paul: 'There is one body and one
Spirit, just as you were called to the one hope that belongs
to your call, one Lord, one faith, one baptism, one God and
Father of us all' (Eph. 4:4–6). Seven marks of unity there,
seven things designed, as he puts it in the previous verse, to
enable us to 'maintain the unity of the Spirit in the bond of
peace'. They may seem a bit arbitrary, but I am not so sure.
All seven spring from the unity of God who has acted on
our behalf. One Father creates the one family worldwide.
One Lord Jesus Christ creates the one faith, the one hope,
the one baptism. One Holy Spirit creates the one Body.
This one God, Father, Son and Holy Spirit, holds out to us
the gift of baptism. So to multiply churches, to repeat
baptism, is as ridiculous as to multiply or repeat God. But
what is this one baptism in which all must share?

Let's pop out into the street, and enquire of the passers-
by. They may well not be able to give any theological
precision to their replies, but they will at least serve to
illustrate the divergence, not to say confusion, which reigns
over this matter of baptism.

Three views

'Excuse me', we say, 'but I wonder if you would mind us
asking you a question? Have you been baptised and, if so,
what does it mean to you?'

The first man we meet turns out to be a practising
Catholic. ' I most certainly have been baptised,' he replies.
'It took place when I was about a month old, and it means a
great deal to me. For it was baptism which brought me into
the Christian church. All I do now as a Christian, all I am,
springs from that baptism into the church long ago.'

If we pursued our enquiries a little farther down the

street, we should be sure, sooner or later, to run into a Baptist. He, too, would have a clear answer to our question. 'Yes, I have been baptised, and properly, by immersion. It was three and a half years ago. I had lived a fairly wild life, but had recently been brought to a living faith in Christ, and my pastor showed me that I should be baptised now that I was a believer. He took me through the Acts of the Apostles, and I saw the point. So I got baptised, and it was marvellous. I can still vividly recall going down into the water, letting it all close over me as if to mark the death and burial of my old life, and then the start of a new life with Christ as I burst out from under the water. It was my public witness to having come to Christian faith.'

Let's go down the road again. We bump into a delightful, enthusiastic character who says something like this, in response to our enquiry. 'Have I been baptised? I most certainly have. As a matter of fact I was christened as an infant, but I don't count that, because I knew nothing about it, and it did me no good. I scarcely had a thought for God in the next twenty-five years. But then I got converted, and went through water-baptism as an adult. That was great, and I don't want to belittle it, but it fades into insignificance compared with the subsequent baptism with the Holy Spirit which happened to me a few months later. This is the baptism which really counts. Life has been very different since then. Have you, I wonder, been baptised with the Holy Spirit?'

Three people. Three quite different views of the one Christian baptism. For the Catholic it marks his continuity with the people of God across the world and down the ages. It is the instrument by which he enters the Christian church. For the Baptist it marks his repentance and faith, his adult response to what God in Christ has done for him. For the Pentecostal, and for many Christians helped through the charismatic movement, the baptism which really counts is the baptism 'in' or 'with' the Holy Spirit, an experience which turns the water of normal Christian experience into wine.

Two steps farther out

Of course, if we had pursued our enquiries a bit farther, we should have met with even more diverse replies. We should have been sure to meet some fringe and nominal adherent of one of the main-line churches which baptise infants. He might be a Methodist, a Presbyterian, a Roman Catholic or an Orthodox. In England he would most probably be an Anglican. He would be surprised at our question, and might well be vague about the answer. But it could well run something like this. 'Yes, I'm almost sure I have been baptised – that is, if it's the same as christening? My mother told me once that she had had me "done" along with the diphtheria jabs when I was a few months old. I don't remember, personally! What does it mean to me? Well, it means I'm Church of England – see? A Christian? Of course. Do I go to church? Well, Christmas and Harvest, you know.'

As if in reaction against this sort of formalism, a Quaker is, appropriately, the next to cross our path. 'Yes, I am a Christian', he says, 'but as a matter of fact I haven't been baptised at all. We in the Society of Friends set great store by the inner light. True religion is not a matter of outward ceremonies, but a stillness of heart before the living God. We see no need for external marks of membership.'

Such an attitude is very understandable. But it is every bit as unbiblical as the formalism against which it reacts. Jesus was very tough on hypocrisy and formalism. But, equally, he did command his followers to 'go and make disciples of all nations, baptizing them in the name of the Father and of the Son and of the Holy Spirit' (Matt. 28:19). I do not for a moment suggest that a Quaker or a member of

the Salvation Army may not be a committed Christian, full
of the Holy Spirit. I am merely saying that in their refusal to
be baptised they are declining to obey the explicit direction
of Jesus.

Those who reject baptism altogether form a very tiny
minority. But what are we to make of the three totally
different views of baptism represented by the Catholic,
Baptist and Pentecostal in the imaginary questionnaire
above? Each of them makes an important point. But what
has happened to the one baptism?

Some years ago Bishop Lesslie Newbigin, the celebrated
missionary theologian, wrote a book called *The Household
of God*. In it he showed how each of the three main
movements in Christianity, the Catholic, the Protestant,
and the Pentecostal, was preserving a valuable strand in
New Testament Christianity, but was inadequate and un-
balanced without taking full account of the other two. All
three strands are to be found in artless juxtaposition in the
pages of the Acts of the Apostles.

The Catholic strand

One strand sees baptism as the gateway into the people of
God, the new Israel, the people on whom God had set his
seal. Just as you entered the old Israel by circumcision, so
you became a member of the new Israel by baptism. The
concluding exhortation of Peter's sermon on the first Day
of Pentecost is a good example of this strand. He calls on his
hearers to 'Save yourselves from this crooked generation'
and we are told that those who received his word were
baptised, 'about three thousand souls' (Acts 2:40, 41). The
allusion is very plain. As in Deuteronomy 32:5, the passage
from which Peter's words are drawn, Israel had become a
'crooked generation'. Though made by the Lord to enjoy
him for ever, they had strayed far from him. Peter calls on

his hearers to separate themselves from Jewish nominalism and identify themselves with the true Israel of God which had been continuous since Abraham. To be sure, there had been much failure and sin, but throughout it all there had been an identifiable work of God through and in his people down the centuries. And baptism is seen by the apostle on this, the birthday of the church, as stepping out with the saints of God down the ages, the thin red line stretching right back to Abraham.

Paul was to put it later, 'As many of you as were baptized into Christ have put on Christ . . . And if you are Christ's then you are Abraham's offspring, heirs according to promise' (Gal. 3:27, 29).

That is a noble view of baptism: entry into the family of God through which he has been working since the dawn of time. But there is a terrible danger in this sort of approach. Strong though it is on the corporate side of belonging, it is weak on the individual response. Strong though it is on the objective element in salvation, it is very weak on the subjective. If you think of baptism as *the* mark of being a Christian, irrespective of any personal belief or commitment, it can degenerate into something very akin to magic.

The Protestant strand

The second strand sees baptism as a seal on profession of faith. The church is the company of believers. Therefore the answer to the Philippian gaoler's question 'What must I do to be saved?' is inevitably 'Believe in the Lord Jesus and you will be saved' (Acts 16:31). This strand is widely represented in the Protestant denominations throughout the world. But, as the very variety of those denominations demonstrates, this view, while strong on personal response, is weak on corporate solidarity. When you see the church as simply the body of explicit believers, you run into problems. What are you to make of the very young, or those who for one reason or another are unable to grasp the meaning of the gospel? Can they not be members of his church? What is more, if you do not share the Catholic's strong conviction of one visible church throughout the world, you find it all too easy to split off and form your own body of believers. It is so much easier that way. The church can then become the society of the like minded. And the unity of the body of Christ is shattered. The history of the past five hundred years illustrates this with embarrassing frankness. But despite all the dangers, it is important to stress that this Protestant emphasis is one vital way of looking at the Christian church and at baptism. If the church is not the body of believers, what earthly good is it? If baptism is not the mark of repentance and faith (or 'conversion' as it is often called for short) then why retain it?

The Pentecostal strand

Until comparatively recent times the Catholic and the Protestant understandings of what the church is and what baptism is were the only two in the field. Now a major third force has appeared. It began in the year 1900, when the Pentecostal movement first emerged. That movement quickly split into several different churches, and has been further altered by the worldwide spread of the 'charismatic' or 'neo-Pentecostal' movement (which allows Christians to embrace a good deal of Pentecostal theology and experience while remaining within their own denominations). The heart of this Pentecostal strand is very important, and as strongly rooted in the New Testament as either of the other two. The church is seen not as the historical community (which can be apostate) nor as the body of those who have expressed their repentance and faith (which can be mere intellectual assent). No, receiving the Holy Spirit is the mark of the church. The baptism of the Spirit is the only baptism worth having. 'Any one who does not have the Spirit of Christ does not belong to him' (i.e. is not a Christian). That is the teaching of St Paul in Romans 8:9. And what this same apostle wanted to know, when he met a handful of Samaritan believers in Ephesus, was, 'Did you receive the Holy Spirit when you believed?' (Acts 19:2). So when the Spirit unmistakably falls on Cornelius even before Peter had finished preaching the gospel to him, that is enough. Peter enquired 'Can anyone forbid water for baptizing these people who have received the Holy Spirit just as we have?' (Acts 10:47).

The church at large needs to be very grateful for this Pentecostal stress on spiritual life as the distinguishing mark of the Christian. They are not satisfied with any rite, any profession, if there is no manifestly recognisable inner reality. And that is great. However it has a real weakness, just as each of the other strands does, if taken in isolation. Cut off from historical continuity it can be (and frequently is) very divisive. And cut off from any emphasis on content it can easily (and frequently does) go off the rails in doctrine or morals. There is such a thing as church history, and it is foolish to neglect its lessons and to suppose one can move straight from the pages of the Acts to the present day as if 2,000 years of history did not intervene! And there is such a thing as Christian doctrine: the Spirit of God and the Word of God need to walk hand in hand if there is to be a balanced Christian life.

They belong together

We find it very hard to hold together these three strands, represented by the Catholic, the Protestant and the Pentecostal movements in Christendom. The earliest church seems to have held them together with comparative ease. For baptism is a big thing. The Catholics are right in seeing it as the seal of a great rescue achieved once for all through the coming and dying and rising of Jesus, a rescue to which we can make no contribution or addition. It is effective *ex opere operato*, in one very important sense of that much misunderstood phrase. It is effective because of what God in Christ has done for us, not because of any action or profession of faith that we make to him. Baptism is the mark of redemption, and that redemption stands whether I appreciate and respond to it or not. For baptism points to the solid, objective nature of God's rescue, and ushers us into the unbroken stream of those who have, down the ages and across the world, made that salvation their own, within the family of the Christian Church.

Yes, baptism is a big thing. For it points also, as the Protestant Churches have clearly seen, to the need for closing with God's offer, of responding to his love, and of surrendering our lives to him. Without that response, there may well be an objective rescue on God's part, but it does me no good. It is as if my favourite aunt went to a dealer and bought me a brand-new Ford, to be collected. If I never went and collected it, I should never be able to make any use of it, however true it was that the car technically belonged to me. Baptism signals that response.

But surely the Pentecostals are right in seeing that you can baptise people until you are blue in the face; that you can recite creeds or sign bases of faith with great energy, and still be a complete stranger to the Spirit of God. And baptism lands you in the world of the Spirit. Unless that has become real to you, your baptism is not what God intended it to be. Baptism is meant to plunge you – no less – into the waters of God's Holy Spirit. Alas, as currently practised, it seems often to be very far from that. Hence the protest and the particular emphasis of the Pentecostals.

So, as we turn from the confusion of modern partial

answers and search in the New Testament, three strands are evident in Christian beginnings. Baptism is meant to denote all three. There is the human side, repentance and faith. There is the churchly side, baptism into the visible family of Christian people. And there is the divine side, forgiveness of sins and reception of the Holy Spirit. All three belong together. All three are necessary parts of Christian initiation. We have become so impoverished in our understanding, and so distanced from one another through our denominational emphases, that we often fail to perceive the need for all three strands in this rope of Christian beginnings. Baptism brings us into the church. Baptism embodies our response to the grace of God. But if we are baptised in water only, and not in the Holy Spirit, we have missed out on the gift of God and content ourselves with the wrapping paper. All three are necessary. If you ask 'which is the most necessary?' that is a silly question. But I suppose the answer would have to be – the divine side, the Holy Spirit. If you ask 'which is the least important strand in that rope?' that would be an even more stupid question, but I suppose the answer would have to be – the churchly side. The truth of the matter is that the three belong together in God's plan for our salvation as surely as loving companionship, sexual relationship, and children belong together in God's plan for our marriage. The 'one baptism' has these three strands to it. Don't be satisfied with less. Don't write off those who stress a different strand from you. A real Christian is a believer in Jesus Christ who has received God's Holy Spirit and has been baptised into his church.

2
BACK TO THE BEGINNING

There was once a professor of church history. When he came to give the opening lecture in his course, his students were amazed to find that he took them right back to Abraham. But of course the professor was quite right. The God who meets us in the New Testament is the same God who for centuries had been making himself known in the Old Testament.

Learning from Abraham

Let's start with Abraham, then. What has he to teach us on the subject of baptism, of all improbable things?

Children of Abraham

In his letter to the Galatians Paul is engaged in arguing with his readers who seemed to think that doing good things, especially keeping the Old Testament law, would bring them to God. He points out that in the new situation brought about by Christ, as well as beforehand, there was only one way in which men were reconciled to God, and that was by God's initiative and achievement. And in the last few verses of chapter 3 of that Epistle he tells them three wonderful things that Jesus Christ has brought them.

Because Christ came, they can be justified by faith (v. 24).
Through faith in Jesus Christ they are all sons of God (v.
26). And as many as were baptised into Christ have put on
Christ (v. 27). Baptism, faith, justification: they all belong
together. They are different aspects of what it means to be
in Christ, different descriptions, if you like, of being a
Christian. And then he ends the chapter in a remarkable
way, remarkable and faintly odd. It seems such an anti-
climax. He says, 'And if you are Christ's, then you are
Abraham's offspring, heirs according to promise' (v. 29).
Why should he congratulate these men and women, raised
to inconceivable heights through their incorporation into
Christ, on being the offspring of a man who had died as a
desert sheikh two thousand years earlier?

Because a very important principle was at stake. It was a
truth that they had clearly not fully understood. If we look
back to Genesis we can get the picture.

A covenant of grace

God's heart was deeply grieved at the sinfulness and rebellion of mankind whom he had made to love him and
enjoy him for ever. He meant the Adam ('man') he made to
'walk with him in the garden in the cool of the day'. Instead,
man did his own thing, disobeyed God, and found his
company irksome – as we always do when we know we are
in the wrong. 'Where are you, Adam?' is God's cry to which
we give no answer. God knows, and we know, that we are
naked. The early chapters of Genesis are full of the fruits of
man's rebellion.

And in this fallen world God was looking for someone
whom he could trust, someone who would trust him. He
found Abraham, and he approached him in sheer, un-
dreamed-of grace. God didn't owe anything to Abraham.
He just loved him. That was all. And Abraham responded

to that love. In Genesis 11 and following, the story begins to take shape. Abraham leaves his home and country in response to God's call, and God promises to give him a land for his descendants for ever. The trouble was that Abraham did not have any descendants, and was now long past the age of begetting children. So in chapter 17 God takes a decisive step. He approaches Abraham and reminds him that he is God Almighty. Nothing is too hard for him. He wants to make a 'covenant', a binding agreement, with Abraham. Abraham was to walk before God in integrity. And God was to make Abraham the father of many nations and give his descendants a very special country to live in.

'Behold, my covenant is with you, and you shall be the father of a multitude of nations . . . And I will establish my covenant between me and you and your descendants after you throughout their generations' (Gen. 17:4, 7).

The mark of the covenant

Incredible stuff, for an old man of 99. He could be pardoned for doubting it. And so God determined to give him a physical mark to assure him that he really did belong, and the Lord really would fulfil his promises, however improbable that fulfilment might seem. So God told Abraham to circumcise himself and all the male descendants that would be born in his house. 'You shall be circumcised in the flesh of your foreskins, and it shall be a sign of the covenant between me and you' (v. 11). There was nothing very special about circumcision. Lots of the surrounding tribes did it, for health reasons. But God took this perfectly ordinary thing and made it a standing mark to Abraham of the reality of the covenant. And Abraham accepted it. He circumcised himself, and Isaac when in due course he was born, and all the males of his household, be they slaves or free. Each one had the mark of the covenant in his flesh. It was very important. 'Any uncircumcised male who is not circumcised in the flesh of his foreskin shall be cut off from his people; he has broken my covenant' (v. 14).

One plan of salvation

This, then, is the pattern of salvation we find as far back as Abraham. Our covenant-making God takes the initiative and approaches Abraham in sheer grace. Abraham responds in faith: 'And he believed the Lord; and he reckoned it to him as righteousness' (Gen. 15.6). The grace of God is met by the faith of Abraham. That is how Abraham was put right with God. That is how you are. There is no other way. There never has been. Do not believe those who tell you that there was one way of salvation in the Old Testament days (lawkeeping), but that God has now changed his mind and decided that faith would be a better idea! Men and women were saved in the Old Testament in just the same way as they were in the New Testament – by the sheer undeserved generosity of God, to which they respond in adoring trust: the grace-faith reciprocal. That is how it has always been with God, and always will be. God's grace: all of him for us. Our faith: all of us for him.

Such is the covenant. And God gives circumcision as a tangible proof of the validity of this covenant between God's free acceptance of Abraham and Abraham's free acceptance of God.

Notice one thing more about this mark of the covenant. It was strictly enjoined, as we have seen, but its efficacy was not automatic. Esau was circumcised, Ishmael was circumcised, but it did them no good. Their hearts were not right in the sight of God. The outer mark did not correspond with the inner reality. Abraham had believed God and had entrusted himself to God without reserve. Not they. The circumcision which was a marvellous mark of reassurance

to Abraham's trembling faith was an embarrassment to the
Esaus and Ishmaels of this world. They had the external
mark, but not the inner disposition.

Application to baptism

All of this is very instructive, if indeed we Christians are
Abraham's offspring. It tells me that the Christian life is
response in faith and obedience to the God who takes the
initiative and comes in sheer grace to seek me out. It tells
me that God generously gives a physical mark of belonging
to seal that unseen contract between his undeserved love
and our wobbly faith. Baptism is obviously the mark of
initiation into the New Covenant, just as circumcision was
into the Old. Indeed, Paul brings the two of these sacramental acts together and links them with the dying and
rising of Christ in his letter to the Colossians. 'You were
circumcised', he tells them, 'with a circumcision made
without hands, by putting off the body of flesh in the
circumcision of Christ; and you were buried with him in
baptism, in which you were also raised with him through
faith in the working of God who raised him from the dead'
(Col. 2:11–12).

Baptism, then, corresponds to circumcision under the
Old Covenant. It is a mark of the covenant or agreement
between God's grace and our response. Not just of his
grace, nor just of our response. It is the seal both on his
initiative and our response. If we are to take seriously the
Genesis story and the strong injunction to circumcise all the
males, whether or not they were old enough to know what
was going on (and you don't know a lot at eight days old!),
there would seem to be some case for baptising the children
of believers, but we shall look at that in a later chapter. The
other point to note at this stage is that if we see baptism as
the fulfilment under the New Covenant of what circumcision

was under the Old, then, like circumcision, it cannot be treated as automatically effective. If the inner attitude of response does not grasp hold of God's loving initiative, then the baptised person in Christian society no more tastes the reality of salvation than did the nominal, circumcised Jew who did not share Abraham's faith.

In short, then, God has one plan of salvation, in which his grace is met by man's faith. Baptism, like circumcision, is the sign of the covenant. And covenant signs are conditional, not automatic.

Learning from Noah

Noah is another Old Testament man to whom the New Testament writers turn for an understanding of baptism. In a remarkable passage in his first letter, Peter refers to

God's patience . . . in the days of Noah, during the building of the ark, in which a few, that is, eight persons, were saved through water. Baptism, which corresponds to this, now saves you, not as a removal of dirt from the body but as an appeal to God for a clear conscience, through the resurrection of Jesus Christ, who has gone into heaven and is at the right hand of God, with angels, authorities, and powers subject to him (1 Pet. 3:20–2).

Peter picks out a number of elements in the story of the Flood (Genesis chs. 6–9) and applies them to Christian baptism.

First, note the background. It is one of judgment and grace. Inevitably God could not remain unmoved when he

saw that the wickedness of man was great in the earth, and that every imagination of the thoughts of his heart was only evil continually. And the Lord was sorry that he has made man on the earth, and it grieved him to his heart. So the Lord said 'I will blot out man whom I have created' . . . But Noah found favour in the eyes of the Lord (Gen. 6:5–8).

God is holy love. He cannot abide sin and must judge it – now as much as then. But the Noahs of this world who trust and obey him find favour in his sight, now as then.

Second, baptism saves you.* That is what Peter says. It is not merely a picture of salvation, but an instrument of it. As he reflected on the story of the Flood he saw an analogy between going to safety through the waters of the Flood, and through the waters of baptism.

Third, the family belongs together. Peter makes particular play with the fact that eight people in Noah's household got to safety in the ark. The Lord is interested in families. They were his idea. He created them and loves them. And his salvation in Scripture often embraces not only the believers like Abraham and Noah, but their families, whether or not they believe as well.

Fourth, baptism is not automatically effective. Far from it. He stresses that it is not the physical act of baptism, 'the washing away the dirt from the body' which saves: it is, rather, something altogether more inward. There is nothing automatic about its efficacy.

Fifth, baptism demands a response. What is this inner something to which Peter alludes? The word used, *eperotēma*, can be taken in more than one way. It could mean the plea in the heart of the candidate for the Lord to cleanse him through and through. But the word was also used of the Roman *sacramentum*, or oath of allegiance, which bound a soldier to the officer enrolling him. In this case it would mean 'the pledge of allegiance coming from an unfeigned conscience'. In either case the element of human response to the divine initiative is clearly stressed.

---

*This statement should not be confused with saying that baptism must be added to repentance and faith as a condition of salvation because baptism is instrumental to salvation not the ground of salvation. Likewise this statement should not be seen as lending credence to the idea that baptism is invalid if it is undertaken without its being intended as a saving act. On the issue of rebaptism, see chapter 8, especially pp. 113-20.—ed.

Finally, the ark is significant. Peter clearly wanted to teach his readers something important through this allusion to Noah's ark. In the ark there was safety: everywhere else was doomed. The same is profoundly true at a spiritual level. Christ is the ark, the only place of safety. Outside Christ I have ultimately no hope, and no security. I wonder whether the New Testament idea of a Christian being someone who is 'in Christ' owes anything at all to this evocative picture of the ark?

Whether or not this last point is justified, the other five show how much the New Testament writers sought and mused over Old Testament stories and themes as they struggled to understand the new thing that God had done for them in Christ. In a world exposed, justly, to the judgment of God, against all hope and expectation we find he is gracious and provides a way of rescue for the utterly undeserving. You enter this place of safety through baptism, you and your family, and yet that baptism is not an automatic instrument. It needs the hand of faith to grasp it, and pledge total allegiance to the Giver.

Learning from Moses

There is yet a third Old Testament character who is brought before us by New Testament writers to illuminate baptism and the salvation it signifies. Paul introduces us to Moses in 1 Corinthians 10:1ff.

Lessons from the Red Sea

This passage forms part of Paul's assault on the Corinthians for their selfishness and folly in eating food that had been offered to idols. They felt so secure in their sacraments and their 'knowledge' that they were prepared to do anything: it could not harm such sophisticated believers as themselves. Paul wants them to realise how fallacious this is. He reminds them of the Israelites in the wilderness. They had felt so secure in their sacraments that they gave way to idolatry and fornication and assumed that it could do them no harm. Twenty three thousand of them, Paul laconically observes, fell in a single day! They had their counterpart to baptism – going through the waters of the Red Sea. They had their counterpart to the eucharist – the heavenly manna in the wilderness. They had all these privileges, presumed on them, and fell. So let the Corinthians, who think they stand, take heed lest they fall (1 Cor. 10:12). That is the thrust of the passage. Baptism and the Communion are no surefire protection against apostasy. Obedience is necessary too, if they are to stay within the covenant. Such is the general thrust of the passage, and it is an important reminder that to rely on the sacrament of baptism while deliberately walking away from God is a beggar's refuge. But the passage has more to say than that.

It suggests that the way to God lay through Christ even in the ages before the incarnation. The supernatural Rock from which they drank was Christ, asserts Paul (v. 4). There was a great deal of discussion about the Rock passage among the rabbis. But Paul asserts that the real sustainer of those Israelites long ago was the one who later became flesh in Jesus of Nazareth. He, he alone, was the way from God and to God, even in those far-off days, yes, even when they could not possibly have known anything about him.

The passage reminds, us, too, that salvation is provided by God, and by him alone. It was the Lord's strong hand which freed the Israelites from Egypt. It was he who led them through the sea and through the desert. Salvation in the Old Testament, as in the New, is the work of God alone. Baptism strongly asserts this. It is something that is done for you, not something you do. The very passivity of being baptised symbolises the fact that God has done all that is necessary to put us in the right with him.

There is a very strong emphasis in this passage on the human response that God looks for. In the case of the Israelites he did not, for the most part, find it. But some responded, in the faith and obedience to which all were called. The message to the Corinthians, and to us, is plain.

There is a strange phrase in verse 2 about being baptised into Moses in the Red Sea. It seems to indicate that they entered into solidarity, into the closest partnership and union, with their leader, Moses, as they went through the sea that had been supernaturally opened, and which the apostle sees as prefiguring Christian baptism. They were united with their leader. That is the point. Baptism into Christ does the same. It unites the believer with his Lord: supremely, as Paul points out elsewhere, with his death and resurrection.

A covenant-making God

Behind each of these Old Testament allusions lies the notion of covenant. God is a covenant-making God. He binds himself by a physical token, as if he could not be trusted! The token to Noah was the rainbow (Gen. 9:8ff). The token to Moses was the passover (Exod. 12). And the token to Abraham, the supreme mark of belonging which continues among Jews to this day, was circumcision.

All three of these great stories of the Old Testament prepare us to understand what the New Testament writers are going to make abundantly plain. God loves us, unworthy as we are. He has found a way to rescue us. His gracious initiative must be met by our adoring and obedient response. That is the covenant. And that covenant has a sign and seal which is intended to assuage our doubts and give us confidence. These are the preparatory lessons about Christian salvation, and baptism which is its pledge, which we learn from the Old Testament. The stage is now set for the coming of John the Baptiser and Jesus.

3
THE BAPTISMS OF JOHN AND JESUS

A century of civil war had ended. The whole known world was under a single government, that of Rome. Greek was spoken in every civilised city. And one people, the Jewish nation, had spread over most of the Empire and were celebrated not only for their commerce but for their monotheism. The stage was set for the next stage of God's self-disclosure. It was time for Jesus. But before him came John the Baptist, his cousin and his forerunner. And John introduced baptism.

The Baptism of John

People were aghast when this strange man, reminiscent of the prophets of old, eating bizarre food and living rough in the desert, descended upon the religious scene of Israel in about AD 27. He came with a scathing indictment of contemporary morals, and a stirring call to repent and 'Prepare the way of the Lord, make his paths straight . . . And there went out to him all the country of Judaea and all the people of Jerusalem, and they were baptised by him in the river Jordan, confessing their sins' (Mark 1:3, 5).

Repentance for the religious

John was the biggest news that had hit Palestine for a very long time. His actions stirred the country to its roots. And the heart of what he did was to baptise.

It is hard for us to understand what a shock this was. Jews were very clear that 'Gentile dogs' were unclean, and whenever any Gentile family wanted to be incorporated into Judaism there was an elaborate ritual in which the whole family went through a ceremonial bath, a *tebilah*, and washed away their pagan impurities. But here was John treating the chosen people as if they were pagans! He told them that they must not presume on being Abraham's offspring. God was perfectly capable of raising up children to Abraham from the very stones. There was one door into the kingdom of God, one only, and it was both low and narrow. It was called repentance.

Preparing for the kingdom

The second noteworthy thing about John's baptism is that it was all part of getting ready for God's kingdom to come. This is an enormous subject which we cannot begin to tackle here, but suffice it to say that the coming of Jesus was a decisive step forward in the advance of God's kingly rule in the world. John saw himself as of no importance. He was simply a voice. And he took up and applied those famous words from Isaiah 40, "The voice of one crying in the wilderness: Prepare the way of the Lord, make his paths straight" (Matt. 3:3). His job was to get men and women ready for the coming of the King. As we have seen, the idea of the covenant was very important to the Jews. When Israel kept the covenant all was well: but the reverse, too, held good. And at the beginning of the first century AD all was clearly not well. The Romans were in power, the moral state of the nation low. All over the land, therefore, people hoped against hope that God would do something about it, that the rule of God would somehow break in and transform the present disastrous state of affairs. John gave body to that hope, and he stressed that repentance alone would fit people to endure the coming day of the Lord. 'The axe is laid to the root of the trees; every tree therefore that does not bear good fruit is cut down and thrown into the fire' (Matt. 3:10).

Real moral change

Just saying sorry would not do. There had to be 'fruit that befits repentance' (Matt. 3:8). When the multitudes asked what this would mean, John was very specific about the real moral change which his baptism implied. 'He who has two coats let him share with him who has none; and he who has food, let him do likewise.' Tax-collectors also came to be baptised, we are told. That is amazing. They were the lowest of the low in the Jewish pecking order. Luke mentions them as if to stress that nobody is too bad to be forgiven if there is real repentance. They asked what it would mean for them, and were told, 'Collect no more than is appointed you.' Soldiers also asked him, 'And what shall we do?' He said to them, 'Rob no one by violence or by false accusation, and be content with your wages' (Luke 3:10–14).

Looking for forgiveness

John's baptism was clearly designed 'for the forgiveness of sins' (Mark 1:4). It went far deeper than ceremonial defilement, for which the Jewish sacrifices were designed. It went to the heart. The heart of man was wicked, and it needed cleansing and forgiveness. That is what the water indicated. It is a universal symbol of cleansing. And that is what everyone needs, if they are to have anything to do with a holy God. We are not told that John's baptism conferred forgiveness. It was, as we shall see below, a preparatory rite. But it was all about the possibility of forgiveness: it was *eis aphesin hamartiōn* 'with a view to the forgiveness of sins'. The one who was to make that all possible was at hand. It is interesting that Matthew, so as to avoid misunderstanding, does not use the phrase 'with a view to the forgiveness of sins' here. He keeps it for the Last Supper when Jesus predicts his atoning death (Matt. 26:28).

John went to some pains to make people understand that his job was not to be the Messiah, not to play the great prophet, but to be the voice announcing the arrival of the main actor on the stage. 'I baptize you with water for repentance, but he who is coming after me is mightier than I, whose sandals I am not worthy to carry; he will baptize you with the Holy Spirit and with fire' (Matt. 3:11; also Luke 3:16). His was a preparatory rite. He sensed that the Coming One would offer a different and more profound baptism.

Water, wind and fire

John was led to weld together three strands from the prophets as he peered into the future that he could only dimly perceive. Ezekiel had combined two of them long ago, water and Spirit. 'I will sprinkle clean water upon you, and you shall be clean from all your uncleannesses, and from all your idols I will cleanse you. A new heart I will give you, and a new spirit will I put within you . . . I will put my spirit within you, and cause you to walk in my statutes' (Ezek. 36:25–7).

John was under no illusion that water could convey forgiveness of sins. In common with the desert community of sectarian Jews at Qumran, who wrote the Dead Sea Scrolls (a community with which he seems to have had some links), John saw washing with water as the preparatory rite, looking forward to the great cleansing and gift of the Spirit which lay in the future (*l QS* 9–10, and 4.24).

To these twin themes of water and wind (in Hebrew and in Greek the same word is used to denote 'wind', 'breath' and 'spirit', and there is often a play on these meanings in the New Testament) John adds fire. Judgment as well as mercy was anticipated in his baptism. The Old Testament had a lot to say about God administering fire, and it means regularly either destruction or cleansing. Daniel 7:10 had spoken of the stream of fire issuing from the throne of God, and once again the men of Qumran picked it up: judgment like molten fire will befall the world in the last day (*l QH* 3.28ff). This passage from Daniel may well have been in John's mind: it became one of the most popular passages for Christians trying to understand who Jesus was. But John could have found just the same concept in the book of Malachi, from which he derived his understanding of his own mission (Mal. 3:1ff). He was preparing the way for the one who 'is like a refiner's fire . . . he will purify the sons of Levi and refine them like gold and silver' (Mal. 3:2, 3). If they do not allow that, then 'the day comes, burning like an oven, when all the arrogant and all evildoers will be stubble; the day that comes shall burn them up, says the Lord' (Mal. 4:1). Perhaps those who came to John for baptism felt, as the waters of the Jordan closed over their heads, a symbol not only of cleansing but of passing through God's judgment. They underwent the symbol of it in repentance, so that they would not have to undergo the awesome reality of it on the Day of Judgment.

Summary

These, then, are the main themes which emerge from the
first real baptism we meet in Scripture. It is a baptism of
repentance. No pedigree, no good deeds could render it
unnecessary; it was indispensable if you were to get into the
coming kingdom. Nobody was too bad to be included in
God's kingdom. Nobody was too good to need baptism. It
demanded repentance and led to a change of life. It was
public and unashamed. It was a pointer to the last judgment: you either underwent God's judgment in symbol in
the Jordan, or you would have to face it for real later on.
And above all it was a preparatory rite. It pointed forward
to Jesus. He would bring in the kingdom which the voice
proclaimed. He would cleanse the conscience and bring the
forgiveness of sins which John's baptism pointed to but
could not offer. And he would fulfil the hopes of prophets
long ago and put the Spirit of the Lord himself into the
hearts of those who came in penitence to ask. What an
amazing first instalment of the baptism teaching of the New
Testament!

The Baptism of Jesus

Identifying with sinners

John the Baptist stands up to his waist in the Jordan: thus
the early paintings in the Catacombs at Rome portray him.
And he is approached by the most famous candidate for
baptism in all history, Jesus. At first it seems strange that
Jesus should have anything to do with a baptism which was
explicitly said to be for the forgiveness of sins. This was felt
to be a difficulty in early times, as is clear from this extract

from the lost non-canonical *Gospel according to the Heb-rews* which Jerome has rescued for us, 'Behold, the Lord's mother and brethren said to him, "John the Baptist is baptising with a view to the remission of sins. Let us go and be baptised by him." And he said, "What sin have I done that I should go and be baptised by him?"' (*Against Pelagius*, 3:2). Early though the *Gospel according to the Hebrews* is, you can see how far it has strayed from the real Gospels. A self-righteousness has crept into the picture of Jesus. It is hard to imagine him speaking like that. No, he came gladly to be baptised by John, and the only hesitation was on John's part 'John would have prevented him, saying "I need to be baptised by you, and do you come to me?" But Jesus answered him "Let it be so now. For thus it is fitting for us to fulfil all righteousness"' (Matt. 3:14–15).

What could that mean? The answer stares us in the face. If Jesus was really going to act proxy for sinful men and women on the cross, he must identify fully with them. And here he is doing just that. It is a dummy run for Calvary. Here is Jesus, who has done no sin, identifying himself with sinful men and women in the waters of baptism, as a picture of what he had come to do, and what would be worked out in blood and tears on that terrible cross a few years later. It is clear that Jesus saw his baptism in this way. In Luke 12:49ff he spoke of the fire (predicted by John and fulfilled after Pentecost) which he came to kindle on the earth, and how he wished it was already burning. And he reflected, 'I have a baptism to be baptized with, and how I am constrained until it is accomplished!' (v. 50). *His cross was to be his baptism!* It was there that he carried in awesome reality the sins of the world which he symbolically identified with when he was baptised by John in the river Jordan. That is the most striking thing about Jesus' baptism. He identified himself with sinners in order, in due time, to bring about the forgiveness of sins to which John's baptism pointed.

Anointing by the Spirit

First, his baptism meant an anointing by the Holy Spirit.
'The heavens were opened and he saw the Spirit of God
descending like a dove and alighting on him' (Matt. 3:16
and parallels). Maybe an actual dove settled on him at his
baptism. Maybe it was a vision. It does not matter very
much. But the important thing is that God's Holy Spirit
came mightily upon him. He was, of course, no stranger to
the Spirit. He had been conceived under the Spirit's in-
fluence (Matt.1:20). But now he was starting out on his
ministry, and Isaiah's prophecy, 'the Spirit of the Lord shall
rest upon him' (Isa 11:2), was being fulfilled. The evangelists saw great significance in this 'resting'. The Holy Spirit
could be withdrawn in Old Testament days. A Saul, a
Samson, might do great exploits in the power of the Spirit,
and then the Spirit might be withdrawn because of dis-
obedience. It would be a marvellous thing if the Spirit came
to rest on someone. And then it happened with Jesus. 'I saw
the Spirit descend as a dove from heaven, and it rested
[remained] on him', said the Baptist (John 1:32). At his
baptism Jesus received a permanent, unwithdrawn endow-
ment of the Holy Spirit. He had come, and he would not
be removed. And that is one of the most precious strands in
Christian baptism. It is the sacrament in which the permanent presence of the Holy Spirit is offered to us. We
may, like Jesus, have had dealings with him before. Subsequently, we may go through barren periods of life when
we are deaf to his gentle voice, and other times when we are
vitally aware of his power. But baptism is the rite in which
his permanent presence in our lives is pledged by God
Almighty, just as it was with Jesus.

Assurance of Sonship

The second strand which is so prominent in Jesus's baptism was his assurance of Sonship. 'This is my beloved Son' (Matt. 3:17 and parallels). Here again, Jesus was already Son of God, but his baptism was the rite in which this Sonship was expressly emphasised. He did not become Son of God at the moment of his baptism: he was Son of God already. But he received a powerful assurance of it. Now, of course, we cannot go directly from the Sonship of Jesus to our own. He was Son of God by nature, we by grace. He was the authentic Son of God: we are only adopted sons because of him. He could cry *Abba*, that intimate word for 'Daddy', by right. We can use it only because he allows us to, and encourages us when we pray to say '*Abba*, hallowed be your name . . .' Yes, Jesus instals us into his very own Sonship. That is one of the most profound meanings of baptism. 'You have received the spirit of sonship,' exults the apostle Paul. 'When we cry "Abba! Father!" it is the Spirit himself bearing witness with our spirit that we are children of God, and if children, then heirs, heirs of God and fellow heirs with Christ, provided we suffer with him in order that we may also be glorified with him' (Rom. 8:15–17).

The path of the Servant

The third strand which the baptism of Jesus brought out is servanthood. The Messianic Son was also the Suffering Servant. That was evident throughout his ministry, and supremely at its end, but it is indicated here at the start. The quotation 'You are my Son, in whom I am well pleased' is a composite one. The first half comes from Psalm 2:7, 'You are my son'. Jesus fulfils and surpasses the intimacy with God that the kings of Israel were meant to enjoy. But the second half of that quotation comes from Isaiah 42:1,

'Behold my Servant whom I uphold, my chosen, in whom
my soul delights'. That is the first of the four 'Servant
Songs' in Isaiah, pointing to the hardship and sacrifice and
death of the Servant of the Lord, and the marvellous
achievements that his death would bring about, culminat-
ing in the famous chapter, Isaiah 53. So in this quotation the
Son, the highest ideal in Judaism, is united with the Servant, the lowest role, which nobody wanted to undertake.
And they are both brought home to Jesus at his baptism.
He, the Son, had to tread the path of the Servant. And so
must his followers. There is a good deal of triumphalism
around in many Christian circles today. We want blessings
now, riches now, healings now, and spiritual gifts now. You
don't hear a lot about the call to suffer and to serve. But
sonship cannot be divorced from suffering and servanthood. They are part of the one baptism.

Enrolled for ministry

The last main strand in the baptism of Jesus was witness-
bearing. Jesus did not simply receive in his baptism a warm
feeling of acceptance and Sonship, a gratifying experience
of the Holy Spirit, and a premonition of servanthood. He
was commissioned for ministry. That commissioning was
immediately followed by a period of prolonged doubts and
testing in the burning wilderness of Judaea for forty terrible
days. And he was taken there by the Spirit who had settled
upon him at his baptism! Reception of the Spirit does not
act as a preservative against hard times. It enables us to
survive them, as Jesus did, and get on with the job. He
came back from the desert sure of his God's provision, sure
of his own calling, sure of the Spirit's leading, and he began
at once the ministry God had assigned to him. He burst
upon the scene in Galilee preaching the gospel of God, and
saying, 'The time is fulfilled, and the kingdom of God is at

hand; repent, and believe in the gospel' (Mark 1:15). That is what he did when the Spirit came upon him at his baptism. It was an enrolment to ministry. And it is for Christians, too. Baptism has been called the ordination of the layman. And in the eyes of the New Testament, we are all laymen. When the Spirit baptised the first disciples into Christ at Pentecost, they immediately began to preach the good news to all and sundry, just like their Master.

The one baptism

The baptism of Jesus, then, while being unique, has much to teach us about Christian baptism. It is the pledge of the Spirit. It is the mark of Sonship. It is the call to the path of the Servant. It is commissioning for ministry.

These are all aspects in Christian baptism, but Christian baptism takes us farther still. It catches us up into the baptism of Jesus, no less. And this baptism of his has three mighty strands woven into it.

First, there was the 'baptism' of repentance in Jordan, administered by John, with which Jesus willingly identified himself on our behalf.

Second, there was the 'baptism' on the cross, where he dealt with the sin of the world and made possible the justification of the ungodly.

Third, there was the 'baptism' of the Holy Spirit, as the Spirit came powerfully on him and equipped him for the ministry.

And we are caught up by baptism into all this. We go down with Jesus into the water of repentance. We claim for ourselves the justification he won on Calvary. And we look to the Holy Spirit to fill us and equip us for ministry. Three strands in the one baptism: three moments in the baptism of Christ. Our baptism is all of that. Let us never forget it.

4
BAPTISM: WHAT DOES IT MEAN AND WHAT DOES IT DO?

What Does Baptism Mean?

Antecedents of Christian baptism

At last we are in a position to understand what Christian baptism means. This sacrament of Christian initiation, which Jesus commanded his followers to practise wherever they went in the world, owes much to the Old Testament, much to the baptism of John and much to the baptism of Jesus.

The Old Testament reminds us that God makes covenants. They are between his grace and our response. He takes the initiative, and we surrender our lives to him in grateful allegiance. He gives us a physical mark of belonging to the covenant. Baptism takes over from circumcision as the mark of the covenant, but the covenant itself remains unchanged: it is between God's grace and our response.

The baptism of John reminds us above all that baptism is meant to bring us in repentance to receive the forgiveness of sins. Otherwise we shall have to face the righteous judgment of God. It points forward to the cleansing and indwelling of the Holy Spirit which Jesus would make possible. Nobody is so good that they do not need this:

nobody is so bad that they cannot receive it. In every case, however, it must mark the start of a new life which involves moral change.

The baptism of Jesus himself takes us much further. It was in this sacrament that he was anointed by the Holy Spirit. It was at his baptism that he perceived his status as Son and his role as Servant. It was here that he received his commission for a life of ministry. Christian baptism includes all these things, because, above all else, it unites our lives with that of Jesus.

The New Testament does not spend a lot of time theorising about baptism. It makes it plain that the early Christians obeyed their Master and went about actually doing it. But in the course of the New Testament there are many explanatory allusions to baptism. Here are some of them, and varied though they are, they all point decisively in a single direction.

Images of Christian baptism

Baptism speaks of new birth (John 3:5). A totally new life begins, which will grow and develop like a baby turning into an adult. But, like a birth, baptism is both necessary and unrepeatable.

Baptism speaks of washing (1 Cor. 6:11). The sin which estranges me from God is washed away in this glorious sacrament. Not, of course, that baptism has power to do this by itself. It takes us back to the supreme baptism, when Jesus Christ dealt with sin once and for all on the cross. This is the baptism he had to be baptised with (Luke 12:50) if we were to be washed. And Christian baptism offers us the fruit of the Lord's baptism at Calvary.

Baptism is more than washing. It is the sacrament of justification. Romans 6:3f stresses this. It is one thing to be washed and forgiven. It is quite another to be justified, to be acquitted, to have the charge-sheet against us so wiped clean that nobody could see that it had ever existed. That is a marvel almost beyond imagining, and it is conveyed to us in baptism. Many Christians of Evangelical persuasion tend to see justification by faith as the very opposite of baptism. Paul sees them as the outside and the inside of the same thing. Both baptism and justification are done for us. Both are for the totally undeserving, and exclude any possible notion of merit on our part. Both launch us into Christ. Both are unrepeatable: you can no more be rebaptised than you can be rejustified. And both are eschatological. They anticipate graphically in the here and now the final verdict of God Almighty on our lives. He looks at us and says, 'That old you has died, drowned in the waters of baptism', just as he looks at us and says, 'The condemning list of all your failings has been erased for ever. It can never be seen nor come to mind.' Yes, baptism is the sacrament of justification by the sheer grace of God. And it is significant that the Reformers saw it thus and did not repeat the baptism they had received as infants.

Baptism is putting on a suit of new clothes. That is what it means in Galatians 3:27 when it says, 'For as many of you as were baptised into Christ have put on Christ.' It is as if we emerge from our old, filthy, tattered clothes, get a thorough bath, and then put on a marvellous, new, beautiful suit of clothes. Jesus is that new suit. And with baptism we put it on.

Baptism is the way of escape from the dangers of the Flood (1 Pet. 3:20f). It is like having the light switched on when you are asleep, or coming to life when you are dead (Eph. 5:14). It is like having water poured over the dry, parched ground of your life (Tit. 3:5; 1 Cor. 12:13). It is like being immersed, sunk into Christ. And the New Testament writers tease out that union with Christ, that immersion in him, with two particularly helpful images. The first is incorporation: the second, death and resurrection:

Incorporation into Christ

Baptism means incorporation into Christ (Gal. 3:27). The whole New Testament unites to stress this, in defiance of Greek syntax! For the phrase which constantly faces us in its pages is 'baptism into Christ' or 'baptism into the name of Christ' (the 'name' being, to the Hebrew mind, the 'person', the 'character', sometimes the 'ownership' of the one named). So baptism is a total commitment which brings us into the most intimate union with Christ, rather as sexual intercourse does for a married couple. It is meant both to symbolise that indivisible union, and to bring it about. Christ did all that was necessary for us through his incarnation, his death, and his resurrection. As a result we can be forgiven, indeed, justified or 'made right' with God: but only as we are incorporated in Christ, only as we are united with the Righteous One. That is why the first half of Romans 5 can be so strong on justification: *Christ for us*. But the second half of that chapter is all about the new Adam, and our incorporation in him: *us in Christ*. The two belong together. Justification would be immoral and impossible if we were not taken up and incorporated into Christ the Righteous One. And baptism is the rite of that entry, the seal on that justification, as the beginning of Romans 6 makes so clear. We are from henceforth 'accepted in the Beloved' (Eph. 1:6). This is a marvellous thought. If we are incorporated by God himself into Christ, his death, his resurrection, his victory, and his endless life, then we can never be the same again. Even if our growth is stunted because of cold winds and poor soil, we remain like branches in a tree. The power and the grace are still there, waiting to be appropriated. He is faithful even though we are not.

All of this underlines how important baptism is. It cannot be thought of as an optional extra, which is how some modern Christians seem to treat it; nor can it be repudiated altogether, as the Quakers and Salvation Army do. To do this is not merely to disobey Christ, but to pin all on faith, to give way to excessive subjectiveness, and to neglect the entering into the solid, objective event of salvation history which baptism denotes.

Dying and rising with Christ

The second image of union with Christ brings us to what is perhaps the most profound of all understandings of the meaning of baptism. It is not only incorporation in Christ. It is union with him in his death and resurrection. Baptism plunges us into the dying and the rising of the Lord Jesus, and this aspect is particularly clearly emphasised by full immersion. 'Do you not know that all of us who have been baptised into Jesus Christ were baptised into his death . . . so that as Christ was raised from the dead by the glory of the Father, we too might walk in newness of life' (Rom. 6:3, 4).

Baptism means death to the person I once was, self-centred, unforgiven, alienated from the life of God. Good-bye to all that. It means that as the waters closed over me in baptism God has closed the account for all my past life. And just as Christ rose from the chill waters of death on the first Easter Day, so you and I rise from the waters of baptism to enter on the new life he gives us, a life that is shared with him, governed by him, a life that will never end. From now on we are called to be what, in God's view, we already are. We must become in actual practice those new creatures who have risen from the waters of death.

And death *means* death. At times it will be devastating: death to your hopes, dreams and ambitions. It may mean death to a work you have built up and seen flourish. It will mean death, all along the line, to self-will. That is what it really means to say, 'I have been baptised'. Therefore I must expect these 'grave' experiences. Life will not be a bed of roses. And when they come, I can cope with them in his power, because I know they are not the end: it is through death that resurrection comes. What is more, in my daily life I can enter increasingly into victorious living because Christ has conquered death. That also is part of the 'I have been baptised' – even if sometimes we have to hang on in grim faith waiting for the resurrection.

Powerful stuff, isn't it? It means that Christian discipleship is essentially a dying and rising life. Baptism points the way. The cross and resurrection lie at its very heart. Baptism pledges my total loyalty to a Lord who bids me come and die. Baptism reminds me that this calling involves dying continually to myself and rising from the death of sin by the power of his indwelling Holy Spirit.

So the whole of the Christian life, in time and in eternity is, in a sense, encapsulated in baptism. The Christian life is the baptismal life, and it is all about dying and rising with Jesus, in this world and hereafter. His dying and rising made it all possible. But we too have 'to die to sin and live to righteousness', as Peter put it (1 Pet. 2:24). That is what Christianity is all about. Baptism is rather like a drop of rain in a meadow on a day when the sun has just come out. It is only a single globule of water, but it refracts all the colours of the spectrum. And in baptism I catch reflected all the blessings of God made available for me in Christ. I catch, too, the command, 'Come, follow me.' In this sacrament God confronts me with total demand, and total succour.

Very well then. How shall we summarise what Christian baptism means? How indeed? It is as easy to summarise the colours of the spectrum! But let's have a go.

1. *Baptism embodies God's challenge to repentance and faith*

The Lord looks at me and says, 'You are foul: you need to be washed. Your heart is hard: I need to renew it. You are proud: you need to be brought low. Indeed, you need to die and to receive from me the gift of a new life. Nothing you do, nothing you are, can deserve this mercy from my hand. I offer it to you freely. But you must change your ways. You must repent. And you must stretch out the hand of faith and ask me to accept you. Fear not, I will . . . if you will.' No baptism can be conducted, be it of adults or infants, without a firm and public profession of this repentance and faith.

2. *Baptism offers the blessings of the covenant*

God comes to us in his free, unmerited grace. We respond in faith and repentance, and baptism signs and seals to us all the blessings of the covenant. Forgiveness, sonship, the Spirit, the new birth, justification, and the promise of life after death. All these covenant blessings are pledged to us in baptism. Baptism, as the old Reformers used to say, 'estates' these blessings upon us. It gives us the title to them.

3. *Baptism plunges us into the death and resurrection of Jesus*

We are brought to the point of death and of new life: death to our old life which had no room for God, and new life that comes when his Holy Spirit enters our hearts. Of course, this dying and rising life, which is henceforth to characterise us, must have its practical outworking in the way we behave. So baptism is the gateway to a complete revolution in morals and lifestyle. From now on our aim is to live out the life of Jesus in our own day and circumstances.

4. *Baptism initiates us into the worldwide Christian church*

It is the adoption certificate into the family of God. It is the mark of belonging, the badge of membership. This is not always entirely obvious in traditionally Christian lands where there is a lot of nominalism, where baptism is the socially acceptable thing, and where it is often performed in semi-private. But we get much nearer to the meaning of baptism when we go into a Jewish or Muslim society, and see what baptism means there. It is extremely costly, and often involves the expulsion of a newly-baptised person from home and country. Sometimes the family holds a funeral service, to show that the baptised person no longer belongs to them in any way. He is, to all intents and purposes, dead. This extreme reaction does not take place if the person is a covert believer, but only if he or she is baptised. For baptism is rightly seen to be the point of no return. It is the definitive mark of leaving the old life and following Christ.

It is important to stress this corporate side of baptism. Nobody is meant to be a Christian on their own. We belong to one another, and the mark of that belonging is baptism. That has an important message for us in our local churches. Baptism is not a solitary thing, marking me out as a Christian on my own. It is a corporate thing, making us part of the Body of Christ, with all the privileges, partnership and responsibility which that entails. It has an important message for our inter-church relationships, too. The Lima declaration of the World Council of Churches in 1982 put it well.

The union with Christ which we share through baptism has important implications for Christian unity. When baptismal unity is realized in one, holy, catholic, apostolic Church, a genuine Christian witness can be made to the healing and reconciling love of God. Therefore our own baptism into Christ constitutes a call to the churches to overcome their divisions and visibly manifest their fellowship.

In the Anglican Cathedral in Geraldton, West Australia, there is an unusual baptistry which brings to the fore these last two aspects of corporate belonging and dying with

Christ. For the baptistry stands in the middle of the main aisle. So anybody baptised in it is inevitably brought into the midst of the congregation. This is eloquent symbolism for stressing the corporate nature of baptism and the responsibility of the congregation for the new member. But the second piece of symbolism is even more eloquent. For the shape of the baptistry is that of a coffin! It points to the fact that we are buried with him in baptism, so that we may be raised to newness of life.

5. *Baptism commissions us for the work of the kingdom*

Just as Jesus was ushered by his baptism into the ministry, so are we. It is God's commissioning for service. For baptism is a sign of the kingdom of God. It is both the demonstration that we have surrendered to him as our king, and it is the uniform of those who are engaged in active service on behalf of the king, to draw his rebel subjects back into his allegiance. When Azariah, Bishop of Dornekal, in South India, took over the leadership of his diocese there were few Christians, drawn mainly from the outcaste class. When he relinquished office there were a quarter of a million. He made a habit, whenever he conducted an adult baptism or a confirmation, of getting the candidate to repeat after him, 'I am a baptised Christian. Woe to me if I do not preach the gospel.' A church with that understanding of baptism is likely to grow!

Such, then, is Christian baptism. It is the rite of entry into the Christian church. It is ineffective until there is repentance and faith, but it stresses the initiative of God. It offers to us all the blessings of the covenant between God's grace and our response. It binds us into a unity of life not only with Jesus Christ but with all baptised believers the world over. And it plunges us into that most profound of mysteries, the dying and rising of Jesus Christ our Lord.

What Does Baptism Do?

It is one thing to have clear views about what baptism
means. It is quite another to understand what it does.
Sometimes people who have been baptised in infancy grow
up into Christ like an opening rose. Sometimes there is no
sign whatever that anything at all happened.

A Catholic answer

As is well known, Catholics treat baptism as effecting what
it signifies. It is a sign of the new birth, and it confers it. This
view has great strength. It is clear and uncomplicated. It
makes good sense of the 'instrumental' language associated
with baptism in the New Testament. But it runs into big
problems. Catholics have to assume that justification is
brought about in baptism. But St Paul asserts it comes by
faith. They have to assume that the new birth can take place
in a person without any sign whatever of a change of life.
That is hard to reconcile with the teaching of the New
Testament. For example, here are five marks of regeneration which we find clearly set out in the first Epistle of John.
A regenerate person does not habitually go on committing
sin (3:9). He believes that Jesus is God's anointed deliverer
(5:1). He lives a holy life (2:29). He loves the company of
brother Christians (3:14). He so wants to please Christ that
he is impervious to pressure from other people (5:4–5).
These are just some of the marks which, John says, identify
the person who 'is born of God'. It is ludicrous to say they
describe vast numbers of people who are baptised. Baptism
may be the mark of the new birth, but it manifestly does not
always ensure it. It did not do so in New Testament times,
either. Simon Magus is a case in point (Acts 8:13, 22f). He
was baptised, but he was still 'in the gall of bitterness and in

the bond of iniquity'. No, baptism does not always effect what it symbolises.

A Protestant answer

On the other hand, Protestants generally treat baptism as merely symbolic. It does not, in their view, normally *do* anything at all. Such a view makes good sense of the hordes of baptised unbelievers all over the world, but it runs away from the 'instrumental' language which the New Testament writers attribute to baptism, which we shall discuss further in the next chapter. Through baptism we are saved; we are buried with Christ so as to share his risen life; we are born again; we put on Christ (1 Pet. 3:21; Rom. 6:3–4 and John 3:5; Gal. 3:27). Nevertheless Scripture itself furnishes examples of baptised people who were clearly not born again (e.g. 1 Cor. 10:1–6) and even someone who was clearly regenerate, like the penitent thief, but was not baptised. How are we to make sense of this tangled situation and these divergent views?

A middle way

We can do so by looking on baptism as the title deeds to the kingdom of heaven, the pledge of God's acceptance, his arms extended to embrace us. It is rather like the marriage service where, after the exchange of vows, the minister pronounces the couple man and wife. That is fair enough, because he knows that the signing of the register will follow in a few minutes, and consummation later on. But if either of these two conditions is missing the couple are *not* married even though liturgically they have been said to be! It is eminently sensible. No normal couple would be so

stupid as to fail to consummate their marriage. In antici-
pation of that consummation the pair are declared to be
married. And if, for some reason, such as sudden illness,
the consummation does not take place for some time, their
marriage could be null and void. But what they would need
to do is not to go through the ceremony all over again, but
to supply the missing part, consummation!

Baptism is very similar. It offers us a wedding certificate
to the Lord Jesus Christ, or, if you prefer, an adoption
certificate into the Father's household. It can properly
therefore be spoken of as effecting what it symbolises. But
it does not do so automatically or unconditionally. We have
to repent and believe. And we have to make room in our
lives for the Holy Spirit.

The Anglican Church, for all the bad pastoral practice
which has sometimes allowed indiscriminate baptism, has
in its formularies maintained a wise and biblical balance
between the Catholic and the Protestant view. Article 27 of
the Thirty-nine Articles of Religion (its doctrinal norm)
says:

> Baptism is not only the sign of profession and mark of
> difference whereby Christian men are discerned from
> others that are not christened, but it is also a sign of
> Regeneration or new birth, whereby, *as by an instru-
> ment*, they that receive baptism *rightly* are grafted into
> the Church; the promises of forgiveness of sin and of our
> adoption to be sons of God by the Holy Ghost are visibly
> signed and sealed.

Notice the balance. *As by an instrument* stresses the general
efficacy of baptism. *They that receive baptism rightly*
stresses that this is far from automatic. Baptism is the
pledge of God's new life. But it is like a seed: it only
germinates when it encounters the water of repentance and
sunshine of faith.

The Gorham judgment

There was a very interesting legal case in the middle of the nineteenth century which clarified the Anglican position. The Bishop of Exeter, Henry Philpotts, refused to institute George Gorham into a living in the diocese because he did not believe that regeneration invariably accompanied baptism. The dispute was so sharp that eventually it came before the Judicial Committee of the Privy Council. In 1850 Gorham won his case, and the position was stated by the Privy Council as follows:

> That baptism is a sacrament generally necessary to salvation, but that the grace of regeneration does not so necessarily accompany the act of baptism that regeneration invariably takes place in baptism; that the grace may be granted before, in or after baptism; that baptism is an effectual sign of grace, by which God works invisibly within us, but only in such as worthily receive it – in them alone it has a wholesome effect; that in no case is regeneration unconditional.

It is an instrument . . . if you receive it aright. Baptism is not unimportant on the one hand, as if we could have done without this mark of the objectivity of the gospel. It is not unconditional, on the other, as if we could presume on its efficacy without making our proper response of repentance and faith.

'All receive not the grace of God', wrote Hooker, that most judicious of Anglican divines, 'which receive the sacraments of his grace'.

Baptism puts you into Christ, if you let yourself be put.

5
THE BAPTISM OF BELIEVERS—
AND THEIR CHILDREN

Is Baptism Necessary?

Salvationists and Quakers are well known for their rejection of both sacraments of baptism and the Communion. But there seems to be an increasing number of people these days who say, 'I know the Lord. What do I need external marks like baptism for?' That is a fair question and it deserves a plain answer.

The answer seems to me to be at least threefold.

The command of Christ

In the first place, there is a clear and unambiguous command of Jesus himself which we must take into consideration. He made baptism part of his final charge to his disciples before he left them. Not only did he promise them his power and his unfailing presence, but he sent them forth on the great commission to 'Go therefore and make disciples of all nations, baptising them in the name of the Father and of the Son and of the Holy Spirit, teaching them to observe all that I have commanded you' (Matt 28:19). It seems an odd way of observing his commands if we reject the command contained in the very same sentence, to baptise! The same command comes in the longer ending of Mark, where Jesus says, 'Go into all the world and preach the gospel to the whole creation. He who believes and is baptised will be saved; but he who does not believe will be condemned' (Mark 16:15). We need to be baptised as a matter of sheer obedience, if we claim that Jesus is in any sense our Lord.

The mark of the church

Second, baptism is the mark of the Christian community. It is and always has been universally practised among Christians, with very few exceptions. In the New Testament baptism is utterly taken for granted. On the Day of Pentecost three thousand people heard, believed and were baptised, thus being added to the Lord and to the community of the infant church (Acts 2:38, 41, 47). And so it continued everywhere you look in the New Testament. Conversion to Christ brought you into the community of Christ, the church. That community had and still has only one badge of belonging: baptism. The New Testament Church knows nothing of an unbaptised Christian. Of course, you can find the bizarre exception, like the dying thief who did not have time or opportunity to be baptised. But you certainly cannot take refuge in the rationalistic argument, 'I am justified by faith in Christ. I do not need to be baptised.' For baptism is the sacrament of justification by faith. Romans 5 which speaks of our being justified by faith in Christ is followed by chapter 6 which speaks of our being united with him in his death and resurrection through baptism (6:1–4). In Galatians chapter 3, being 'justified by faith', becoming 'sons of God' and being 'baptised into Christ' are all given as alternative and interchangeable descriptions of Christian initiation within three verses (Gal. 3:24–7). Precisely the same point arises from Paul's impassioned plea to the Corinthians for Christian unity. How can they say, 'I belong to Paul' or 'I belong to Apollos' when it is Christ who had been crucified for them, preached to them, and Christ was the one in whom they had been incorporated through baptism? (1 Cor. 1:12ff).

The power of the sacrament

The third reason why baptism is necessary for Christians is even more cogent. It is baptism which grafts us into both Christ and the Christian church. We must resist the tendency, common in Baptist circles but by no means confined to them, to regard baptism primarily as a *witness* to conversion. In the New Testament it is much more clearly identified as an *instrument* of conversion. You are not a Christian until you are baptised.* Whether you look at the three thousand on the Day of Pentecost, the conversion of St Paul, that of the Ethiopian eunuch, of the Samaritans, of the Ephesian dozen in Acts 19, of Cornelius or of the Philippian gaoler, the pattern is uniform: baptism is part of the evangelising event, not a subsequent witness to it. The New Testament churches had no probationary period for those working up towards baptism. They repented, believed and were baptised. Baptism is how the church extends its frontiers. It is not a witness, nor a reward: it is an *initiation*, and in the New Testament that point is stressed again and again. Thus the New Testament writers can use strongly instrumental language for baptism, language which makes many Evangelical Christians, brought up to regard baptism as a witness to faith, very uneasy. But look at the force of these quotations. It is through baptism that you enter the 'name' of the Trinity (Matt. 28:19), through baptism that you are born again (John 3:5), through baptism that you are saved* (1 Pet 3:21), through baptism that you get buried in Christ's death and raised with him in

---

*Again, this should not be confused with the idea that baptism must be added to repentance and faith as a condition of salvation. While baptism is necessary and instrumental, it is not a ground of our salvation.—ed.

resurrection (Rom. 6:3ff; Col. 2:12), through baptism that you get incorporated into the one Christian body (1 Cor. 12:13). To be sure, several of these references mention the Holy Spirit (the divine agency) and faith (the human agency), but there is an undeniably instrumental aspect to baptism which Catholics have been very happy with, and which has caused some embarrassment to Evangelicals. There need be no embarrassment! Baptism, justification by faith, becoming a child of God, regeneration – these are all different aspects of Christian beginning. And the sign and seal of that is baptism. Let nobody despise it.

To be sure, baptism is not invariably efficacious. It was not with Simon Magus (Acts 8:13, 21ff). It was not with many of the Corinthians (1 Cor. 10:1–6). It is not with many today if baptism has lost all relationship with actually beginning the Christian life and is treated as a charm or a social convenience. There are conditions to its efficacy, and these are repentance and faith on our side and the gift of the Holy Spirit on God's side. Baptism is efficacious in bringing a person into the Christian church and into Christ, but it is not *unconditionally* efficacious. That is the clear teaching of the New Testament. And that is why it simply will not do either to invest with magical powers or to devalue this sacrament which Jesus left us to mark our initiation and assure us of our belonging. In moments when our faith sinks in the morasses of doubt, we can take heart. God has acted decisively (and physically) for us in Christ. We have been baptised into him, and we belong, however rotten we may feel at any given time.

The Baptism of Believers

Very well, baptism is a necessary part of Christian initiation. But who should be baptised? It is plain from the New

Testament that adult believers should be baptised when they come to faith in Christ, and there is a very strong case for doing it straightaway, otherwise the instrumentality of baptism slips away and it begins to be seen as a witness to something else! Colin Buchanan in *Infant Baptism under Cross Examination* (a debate with the Baptist, David Pawson) reiterates a powerful point he had made previously that 'The New Testament Churches had no catechumenate, no probationary period, no course of instruction prior to admitting adults to baptism – they were admitted the moment they professed faith in Jesus as Lord' (p. 20). This holds good of all the cases in the New Testament, and it is a most important principle. It gives full play to the instrumentality of baptism, and it means that people who have entered into the covenant are not made to wait for its sign and seal.

In our Anglican Church in Oxford we have a large number of adult conversions every year, and many baptisms. The new believer is put straight into a nurture group, and is baptised as soon as possible. As Buchanan amusingly suggests, Billy Graham should hire the Empire Pool for his crusades as well as Wembley Stadium! There is no biblical precedent for asking people to come forward at the end of a time of preaching, raise their hands or receive a booklet. But there is abundant biblical evidence to show that in apostolic days people were baptised forthwith, and this helps us to understand the significance of the New Testament's 'instrumental' language about baptism. It is regarded as generally efficacious.

It is not, however, invariably or unconditionally efficacious, as some extreme sacramentalists would suggest. Interestingly enough, Gorham, in his celebrated dispute with the Bishop of Exeter in the middle of the nineteenth century over the question of the invariable regeneration of infants in baptism, took as his starting point the fact that not all adults who go through baptism are regenerate (even though they undergo a rite which says they are!). But while baptism is not automatic in its efficacy, that is still a far cry from being a mere witness or outward symbol. It is normally seen as effecting what it proclaims, the new birth of the candidate. And this realist language is easier to understand because baptism was usually administered immediately upon profession of faith. Thus repentance, faith and baptism took place in one fell swoop, and the candidate was henceforth a member of the new society, the church.

There is, therefore, no problem about adults coming to baptism. Like Abraham, they respond to the grace of God which is proffered to them in the gospel, and they receive the mark of the covenant which binds them to the Lord. To be sure, the later church determined to have a probationary period before baptism after adult profession of faith, and people argue the pros and cons of that. I have told you my own preference and practice. Let others do otherwise if they so wish. It is not a matter of great importance.

But what *is* a matter of great importance is whether we should allow baptism to a wider circle than adult believers. Are children appropriate recipients of this sacrament? This is a question which is a hot issue today, and has been in some circles since the Reformation. Small children cannot repent, nor can they believe. On what grounds, therefore, can they be baptised?

The Baptism of Infants

Should children be baptised?

The answer of the Baptists, the Open Brethren, and many of the House Churches in Britain and fast-growing independent churches overseas is that there is no adequate ground for baptising infants. It is a scandal. It makes for gross nominalism. It inoculates people against the gospel by making them think that they are Christians when they may be nothing of the kind.

On the other hand, the vast majority of churches in Christendom do baptise the children of believers. The Roman Catholics and the Orthodox, the Presbyterians and the Methodists, the Anglicans and the Closed Brethren, the Lutherans and the Calvinists all baptise the children of their members. They may all be wrong. But there must be some reason for their action. What is it?

There are in fact at least seven considerations which have persuaded most churches down the ages to baptise the children of believers. These arguments are of different weight, but taken together they present a formidable case. No text settles the matter either way. We are not told in Scripture to baptise infants, as most churches do. Nor are we told to dedicate them, as most Baptist churches do. So let us try to lay aside prejudice, and look at the evidence which has led most churches apart from the Baptists who began in the sixteenth century, the Open Brethren who began in the nineteenth century, and the House Churches who began in the middle of the twentieth century, to extend baptism to their children.

1. Children were admitted into the Old Testament Church. As we have seen, God makes covenants. They all spring from his grace, and need to be grasped by human faith and obedience. God's covenant with Abraham was normative for the whole people of God in the Old Testament. His adult response to the grace of God was sealed with circumcision, the mark of the covenant: just like believer's baptism. But it did not stop there. Isaac was born into the covenant community, and he received the seal of circumcision long before he could make any response to God's grace. 'Abraham circumcised his son Isaac when he was eight days old, as God had commanded him' (Gen. 21:4). This circumcising of infants was no occasional aberration, no exception to the normal rule of adult circumcision. It was part of the purpose of God for the family. It was specifically commanded. It was an original and essential part of the covenant that God struck with Abraham before Isaac, the child of promise, was born.

This is my covenant which you shall keep, between me and you and your descendants after you: Every male among you shall be circumcised. You shall be circumcised in the flesh of your foreskins, and it shall be a sign of the covenant between me and you. He that is eight days old among you shall be circumcised; every male throughout your generation, whether born in your house, or bought with your money from any foreigner who is not of your offspring, both he that is born in your house and he that is bought with your money, shall be circumcised. So shall my covenant be in your flesh an everlasting covenant. Any uncircumcised male who is not circumcised in the flesh of his foreskin shall be cut off from his people; he has broken my covenant (Gen. 17:10–14).

Now that is strong stuff. It tells us that the child born into a believing home has the right to the mark of belonging, even when he is too young to fulfil the conditions on which the covenant was made in the first place. It tells us that this position for children is an express part of the will of God. It tells us that the faith of the head of the house is highly significant for his whole household, be that his natural household or others who have, for one reason or another, come under his roof. And it tells us that to refuse to give to infants born within the covenant the sign of that covenant is a very serious fault.

All this is highly relevant to the baptism of children, and their reception into the New Testament Church. Although for Abraham circumcision was the 'sign or seal' on his faith (Rom. 4:11) that sign or seal was applied by God's specific command to Isaac and others like him, born within Abraham's house, but as yet quite incapable of faith. They were circumcised simply and solely because, in the gracious purposes and plan of God, they had been born into a believing family. It is hardly surprising, therefore, to find Peter saying on the Day of Pentecost, 'The promise is to you and to your children' when he challenges his hearers to baptism. 'So those who received his word were baptised' (Acts 2:39ff).

Children were admitted into the Old Testament Church. Are they to be excluded from the New Testament Church? Has God grown less gracious with the passing of the years? Are children meant to be worse off under the New Covenant than they were under the Old? Does a church consist only of consenting adults? Of one thing we may be fairly certain. A Jew, coming over to Christianity and thus fulfilling his Judaism, would be amazed to hear that his children should not receive the sign of the covenant. 'If they can receive circumcision,' he would say, 'why not baptism? If they were welcomed into the Old Testament Church, why not into the New?'

2. The whole family was baptised when proselytes came over into Judaism. When a family came over into Judaism from some pagan background, three things took place. The head of the family offered sacrifices. The males in the family were circumcised. And everybody – but everybody – was baptised. They sat in a bath and baptised themselves, 'washing away Gentile impurities'. Proselyte baptism was pre-Christian. The Pharisees, we are told, 'traverse sea and land to make a single proselyte' (Matt. 23:15). And there is no doubt that proselyte baptism influenced Christian baptism, despite the enormous differences between the two. The language the rabbis used of the newly baptised proselyte is most instructive. He is 'like a newborn child', 'a new creation', 'raised from the dead', 'born anew'. His 'sins are forgiven him'. He is now 'holy for the Lord'. Professor

Jeremias, who goes into fascinating detail on this matter in his book *Infant Baptism in the First Four Centuries*, concludes a careful comparison of the language used in proselyte and in Christian baptisms by observing:

> It is worthy of notice that in these correspondences we have not merely individual points of contact, but that the whole terminology of Jewish conversion theology connected with proselyte baptism recurs in the theology of primitive Christian baptism. Chance coincidence is wholly inconceivable; the only possible conclusion is that the rites are related as parent to child (p. 36).

He goes on to show that not merely in the language used, but in the actions enjoined there is a very close link between proselyte baptism and Christian baptism. In both cases, immersion was preferred, sin was confessed if the person was old enough, and even rituals like women letting down the hair and laying aside ornaments were practised in Christian and in proselyte baptism alike. This should not surprise us. The only model the earliest Christians had for baptismal practice was proselyte baptism, with which they would have been quite familiar. This being so, would it not have been unthinkable for them to have excluded children from baptism? The tiniest children went through the proselyte bath, even sometimes on the day of their birth. Indeed children were admitted to baptism even when only one parent joined Judaism. It is hard to suppose that infants were debarred from Christian baptism which plainly owed so much to proselyte baptism.

The Jewish people rated the family very highly. Both in the case of circumcision and proselyte baptism the place of the whole family is significantly high. It was deeply rooted in their religious life. It would have taken a clear command from Jesus to have stopped it. No such command can be found.

Normally I suspect arguments from silence. But when Jesus, the fulfiller of Judaism, came to a people who for thousands of years had been admitting Jewish children into the covenant at the express command of God to Abraham, their founding father, and when for a long time they had been admitting the children of Gentile converts by baptising them along with all the rest of the family – then the argument from silence becomes rather formidable. Is it conceivable that if Jesus had meant to change this age-old procedure he would not have given some slight indication that from henceforth children were to be treated differently? Should he not have said in the Great Commission, 'Go and make disciples of all nations, but make sure that you baptise only adult believers in the name of the Father and of the Son and of the Holy Spirit'?

3. Whole families were baptised in New Testament days. We read of Lydia's household being baptised (Acts 16:15), of the Philippian gaoler's household being baptised (16:33), of Cornelius' household (11:14) and of Stephanas' household being baptised (1 Cor. 1:16). These passages, introduced artlessly and unselfconsciously into the New Testament narrative, often cause some embarrassment in Baptist circles. They rather hope that there were no small children in the families concerned! But surely this is to fail to give sufficient weight not only to the practice of infant circumcision and infant proselyte baptism but to the whole solidarity of the family in the ancient world. We have become so infatuated with individualism that we find this hard to appreciate. But in the ancient world, when the head of the family acted, he did so for the whole family. Where he went they went. All through the Bible we see God dealing with families, Abraham and his family, Noah and his family and so forth. Perhaps it is only the head of the family who expresses faith, but the whole family receives the mark of belonging. The Philippian gaoler provides us with a good example of this. He asked Paul and Silas

'"What must I do to be saved?" and they said "Believe [singular] in the Lord Jesus and you [singular] will be saved, *you and your household* . . ." And he took them the same hour of the night, and washed their wounds, and he was baptised at once *with all his family* . . . and he rejoiced with all his household that he [singular] had believed in God' (Acts 16:30ff, my italics). The conversion and baptism of the father are grounds for the baptism of all that are in his household, so strong is the solidarity of the family. It brings them all within the covenant. Maybe that is what is meant by the much disputed verse 1 Corinthians 7:14; but I do not propose to use it because baptism is not actually mentioned in that passage which declares the children of believers to be 'holy'.

The solidarity of the family in baptism, as in all else, is the decisive consideration. Of course it does not mean that every member of the family was saved. Neither theology nor experience suggests anything of the kind. But it does mean that all members of a believer's family had the right to the mark of the covenant until they made up their own minds whether or not to respond to the God who had taken the initiative and held out the olive branch of reconciliation towards them. It is greatly to the credit of Kurt Aland, a distinguished Baptist theologian, that he concedes this. 'The house is saved when the head of the house is saved' (*Did the Early Church Baptize Infants?*, p. 91).

This positive evaluation of children springs from Jesus himself. Hence the fourth consideration which bears upon the baptism of little children.

4. Jesus accepted and blessed children too young to respond. In Mark 10:2–16 and parallels we find a most instructive story which shows the attitude Jesus had to children. Quite likely this incident took place on the eve of the Day of Atonement, for on that evening it was a custom, so the rabbis tell us (*Sopherim* 18:5), for pious Jewish parents to bring their children to the scribes so that they could lay their hands on them in blessing and pray that they might one day 'attain to the knowledge of the Law and to good works'. Some parents apparently came to Jesus seeking his blessing. The disciples, perhaps because the parents seemed to be putting Jesus on the same level as the scribes, told them to go away. Jesus was indignant (the word *ēganaktēsen* is very strong and is nowhere else used of Jesus' reactions). He said, 'Let the children come to me, do not hinder them; for to such belongs the kingdom of God. Truly I say to you, whosoever does not receive the kingdom of God like a child shall not enter it. And he took them in his arms and blessed them, laying his hands upon them' (Mark 10:14–16).

Now at first sight this passage has nothing whatever to do with baptism. Nevertheless from the second century onwards it was used to justify infant baptism. Tertullian shows that the words were so interpreted in his day (*de Baptismo* 18:5), and the *Apostolic Constitutions* (6:15) base the practice of baptising children on the words, 'Do not hinder them' (a phrase which had a lot of mileage in baptismal discussions; to 'hinder' became a technical term for refusing baptism). However that may be, there is no overt application of these words to infant baptism in the Gospel. One would not expect it. After all, Christian baptism had not been inaugurated at the time. Much more important is what the passage reveals of Jesus's attitude to children. And note that these were *little* children; the evangelists go out of their way to stress this. Mark's word is *paidion*, a diminutive of the word for child. Luke's is *brephos*, a word which originally means embryo and comes to mean tiny infant. How did Jesus act towards such little people? This passage makes three things abundantly plain.

First, Jesus loves tiny children. He welcomes them to himself, and he blames those who would keep them away.

Second, Jesus is willing to bless them even when they are far too young to understand.

Third, tiny children are capable of receiving a blessing at the hands of Jesus. Who can doubt that when he blessed them they were blessed indeed?

If these things were so, if tiny children were the objects of Jesus's love, were brought to him for blessing when they were too young to understand, and were capable of receiving a blessing from his hands, is it any wonder that the passage was later applied to baptism and that it became natural to bring children into the covenant of grace from the very earliest days of their lives?

Before we leave this fascinating passage, it is worth noting that not only did Jesus bless the children, but he made them a model for all believers. You have to become a child, a trusting defenceless child, lying in Jesus's arms, if you are to profit by the Day of Atonement and enter into the kingdom of God. Far from being exceptions to normal membership of the kingdom, tiny children show us the way in!

5. The church down its history has baptised children. There seems little doubt that it was the established practice of the subapostolic church to baptise infants within Christian homes. About AD 215 the Roman theologian Hippolytus, in a document significantly called *The Apostolic Tradition*, refers in the most natural way to the baptism of children. Indeed, he alludes to it as an 'unquestioned rule'. 'First, you should baptise the little ones. All who can speak for themselves should speak. But for those who cannot speak, their parents should speak, or another who belongs to their family.' Then the grown men were baptised, and finally the women (*Apostolic Tradition*, 21). Hippolytus' order of service for baptism had wide circulation, was translated into various languages, and set the standard for more than a thousand years.

We do not have much explicit evidence before Hippolytus. This is largely because not a great deal of reference is made to baptism in the surviving literature of the second century, and what there is does not always specify whether infant or adult baptism is meant. But what evidence there is supports the unquestioning acceptance of infant baptism. Thus Polycarp (*c.* AD 69–155), himself, it appears, a child of Christian parents, declared at his martyrdom, 'Eighty-six years have I served Him, and He never did me any wrong . . .' This takes us back to around the year AD 70, in the heyday of the young church's advance, when apostles were still alive. It is almost incredible that Polycarp means us to understand that he came to Christian beginnings in baptism as a lad of 12 or 14, when he would have been old enough to make his own adult decision for Christ. Had that been the case he would have been 100 when he died. Not many people reached that age in those days! When they did, it was a matter for special comment. No, Polycarp was almost certainly baptised as a baby eighty-six years before his martyrdom.

The same was true of Origen. Three times he mentions the baptism of infants as a custom of the church, and in his *Commentary on Romans* 6:5–7 he says, 'For this reason the Church received from the apostles the tradition of baptising children too'. Origen, that extremely erudite Church Father, was born in AD 185 to a Christian family, and if he thinks infant baptism was an apostolic practice, he must surely have been baptised as an infant himself. Where did his parents get the idea from? Such questions take us back into the first Christian century.

Another of the great teachers of the early Church, Irenaeus (AD 130–200) is no less clear, and no less relaxed about the practice. He says that Jesus came to save all who through him are born again to God – infants, children, boys, youths and old men. He passed through every age, becoming an infant for infants, thus sanctifying infants, and so forth (*Adv. Haer.* 2:22:4). And Justin (AD 100–165), one of the earliest Christian writers from whom any substantial literary works have come down to us, mentions 'many men and women of the age of sixty and seventy years who have *been made disciples* of Christ [note the passive form, *emathēteuthēsan*] from childhood' (*1 Apol.* 15:6). This is a clear allusion to baptism at a very early age.

The picture is clear and uniform. The early Christians baptised the children in their families, and took this to be an apostolic practice. There is, I believe, only one voice raised against the practice during the first fifteen hundred years of the church's history, the lone voice of Tertullian (AD 160–220). That is not to say, of course, that there were no reformist movements in the church during that millennium and a half. Of course there were. Montanism in the second century, Donatism in the fourth, and the Franciscans, the Hussites and the followers of Wycliffe in the latter part of the Middle Ages were all preparing the way for the Reformation. They were all, in one way or another, attacks on the errors of the institutional church. But they did not bring into question the propriety of baptising the children of believers.

Tertullian, however, did. He lived in North Africa, and in the *de Baptismo*, written in AD 205, he expressed his doubts about infant baptism. It is very interesting that he does not use what would have been a clinching argument against it, namely that infant baptism did not derive from the apostles. He cannot do that, for he knows very well that it is no novelty in the church. Instead, he argues that the baptism of little children, except in cases of dire necessity, imposes too great a responsibility on the godparents; they might die and so be unable to fulfil their obligations, or undesirable tendencies might appear in the children! So he advises postponement of baptism. He prescribes the same for unmarried young adults and widows. Let them wait 'until they either marry or make up their minds to continence'. Tertullian does not contest the legitimacy of baptism for such people, only the wisdom of it. *Cunctatio baptismi utilior* is his conclusion: delay of baptism is more beneficial (*op. cit.*, 18). Ten years later, when writing the *de Anima*, Tertullian is happy for the baptism of children even if one parent is not a Christian, on the basis of a combination of 1 Corinthians 7:14 and John 3:5 (*op. cit.*, 39).

This curious inconsistency in his treatment of infant baptism is probably best explained as follows. He seems to attest the universality of infant baptism, but in the *de Baptismo* reflects the growing tendency towards wanting a 'pure church', which led to a long catechumenate for adults who often deferred their baptism to their death beds! As Colin Buchanan acutely observes, 'a catechumenate or long probationary period before adult baptism entails a reaction against infant baptism; and the apostolic way of doing adult baptism (i.e. immediately on profession of faith) happily accepts infant baptism'. At all events, the inconsistency is clearly there in Tertullian. But his seems to have been the only voice raised against infant baptism. Whatever doubts he had about the propriety of baptising infants, nubile women, and widows before they had had a chance to prove themselves, these doubts made no impression on the North African Church to which he belonged. At the Synod of Carthage some years later, sixty-seven bishops from all over Christian Africa decided unanimously not to defer baptism until the eighth day, as was the case with circumcision, but to baptise directly after birth. So sure were these early Christian leaders that the baptism of infants represented the mind of God as displayed in the Old Testament and the attitude of Jesus.

Before leaving this subject of the early history of the church, one other matter is important. Just supposing the second century church had changed the rules, and had restricted baptism to those who were fully aware of what they were doing, should we not have heard something about it? When in the middle of the first century the Gentile

Church saw no need to insist on circumcision and lawkeeping as conditions of entry into the family of God, there was
a tremendous debate about it, which has left traces not only
in Acts 15 but in many other places in the New Testament.
The reverberations of that discussion were enormous. Are
we to suppose that a change of equal, if not greater,
proportions took place in the early part of the second
century without anyone in the surviving literature referring
to it at all? That would surely strain credulity too far. The
evidence suggests that the apostolic church baptised infants
born to their members, and that this practice continued
throughout the period of the undivided church until the
Anabaptist protest at the Reformation.

6. Infant baptism stresses the objectivity of the gospel. It
points to the solid achievement of Christ crucified and
risen, whether or not we respond to it. Baptism is the
sacrament of our adoption, our acquittal, our justification.
Not that we gain anything from it unless we do what it
presupposes, namely repent and believe. But it is the
standing demonstration that our salvation does not depend
on our own very fallible faith; it depends on what God has
done for us. Infant baptism reminds us that we are not
saved because of our faith but through the gracious action
of God on our behalf which stands, come wind come
weather. And that is a most important emphasis. Martin
Luther, that great advocate, one might almost say re-
discoverer, of the blessings of justification by faith, used to
be beset by the most frightening doubts. At such times he
did not say, 'I have believed'. He was too unsure of his faith
to do that. He said, 'I have been baptised' (as an infant,
what's more!). Baptism stood for what God had done for
him to make him accepted in the Beloved. It was healthily
objective. In our own day, when feelings are so often
mistaken as the barometer of spiritual wellbeing, we could
do worse than learn from Luther.

7. Infant baptism stresses the initiative of God in

salvation. All agree that baptism is the seal on the covenant between God's grace and our response. But you have to administer this sacrament at some time or other. Should it be attached primarily to man's response, or to God's initiative? That is the heart of the question. It is here the paedobaptists (i.e. those who baptise children) and Baptists take different roads. The Baptist believes baptism is improper until a person believes, because he attaches the covenant seal primarily to man's response. The paedobaptist position, which has been the mainstream of Christian thought, takes a different view. Yes, response is important, vitally important. Room must be made for that, in some such sacramental act as confirmation. But, supremely, baptism is the mark of God's prior love to us which antedates our response and calls it forth. For the Baptist, baptism primarily bears witness to what *we do* in responding to the grace of God. For the paedobaptist, it primarily bears witness to what *God has done* to make it all possible.

A letter on infant baptism – theology

I had a letter the other day from a member of our congregation who knew I was writing this little book. He wrote:

I have come to see that all baptism is the sign of what God has done and will do, rather than what we do. It is primarily a testimony to God's promises in the gospel rather than a testimony to our faith. This has helped me to see the unity of Christian baptism irrespective of the age of the recipient.

My impression is that Christians who accept infant baptism, but without such an understanding, really tend to see it as something different in kind from adult baptism, and only the same in name. By accepting a Baptistic understanding of adult baptism as primarily a public profession of faith and an act of obedience, they are hard put to justify infant baptism (as opposed to infant dedication) except on grounds of mere tradition or an extreme sacramentalism.

This type of paedobaptist really agrees with his Baptist brethren that what is going on in the two instances is essentially different because of the obvious differences in the human subjects. If someone has never been taught to view baptism with reference to what God is doing through the rite, it is not at all surprising that he will think about 'declaration' exclusively in terms of the believer's declaration, or the parents' declaration, or the church's declaration of faith – rather than God's declaration of his acceptance and justification of sinners.

I hope your book will help all Christians to understand their own baptism better. I hope it will help Christians who accept both 'convert-baptism' and 'covenant-children-baptism' (my own terminology) to see that they are the same in declaring God's gracious promises in the Gospel (and so to be delivered from both an essentially Baptistic approach to adult baptism and either a sentimental or a magical belief in infant baptism). I hope it will help Baptist Christians to a more God-centred understanding of baptism (and so to be delivered from a man-centred exposition of believer's baptism and a critical attitude towards the baptism of children of believers). May the Lord give you clear words and an irenic spirit.

A lovely letter, I thought. Shrewd and warm. He understands very clearly that there is one baptism, whatever the human recipients, and that it is the sign and seal on God's work for us even more than on our response to him.

A letter on infant baptism – experience

I will close this chapter by quoting another letter, from a person my wife and I know well, who had had a good deal of trauma in the earlier periods of her life.

My frame of mind is infinitely better than it has been for years, largely because of the culmination of a long term healing process. In September I had prayer for inner healing that seemed to remove a major blockage. My mother had told me in August that I had been hospitalised at the age of three months for colic. Not only was this during the era when parents were not allowed to visit children's wards, but also my mother had had to leave the city because my grandfather was dying of heart disease. This was certainly one of the roots of my fear of rejection.

The interesting thing was that when we came to the step of picturing Jesus entering the scene, that was not the picture the Lord gave me at all. Instead, I had a vivid picture of my baptism, which happened shortly after that illness. I could picture myself being held in the minister's arms, which were strong and secure, and being surrounded by light. In fact the sense was that I was being immersed in liquid light which flowed into me and through me, filling all the gaps and healing all the hurts. My infant self *knew* that Jesus claimed me as his own, and that he would never leave me nor forsake me. It was just incredible. This baptism was *the real thing*!

The first letter embodied argument for infant baptism. The second gave personal experience. It is, I believe, a combination of argument (such as the seven we have looked at above) and experience which has led the majority of Christian Churches to continue the Old Testament practice of admitting children into the believing community, as well as adults who come to repentance and faith. There are, however, many objections to this view which makes room for infant baptism, and we shall address them in the next chapter.

6
OBJECTIONS CONSIDERED

In circles which take their Christian commitment seriously there is a great deal of hesitation about the baptism of infants. We shall look at some of these criticisms and questions in this chapter, but there is one point to make clear at the outset. No argument can be produced against infant baptism which does not equally hold good against infant circumcision. While we have no direct command in the New Testament Scriptures to baptise infants we have repeated and explicit commands in the Old Testament Scriptures to circumcise infants. And the same God is the author of both Testaments. Had he changed his mind, would he not have told us?

Let us, then, turn to some of the most important objections to the practice of infant baptism.

1. *'You fail to realise the discontinuity between the Old Testament and the New'*

A Baptist friend who read this book in manuscript and made kind criticisms and suggestions, from which I hope I have profited, wrote this:

The problem with this manuscript from the Baptistic perspective is that it fails to give weight to the breaking of the old covenant and its replacement by the new (cf.

Heb. 8:6f, 13; 9:1, 15, 18). The whole rise of individualism and the new spiritual qualifications required of people of the new covenant is not really taken seriously. If we equate, without reserve, old Israel with the church, then to be logical the church has to embrace the unregenerate, the unbelieving, and the unconverted in its membership.

He makes three points.

First, the breaking of the Old Covenant and its replacement by the New. It is very important to be clear on this. God has always had one way only of relating to human beings. It is a covenant between his gracious initiative and man's adoring response. That was how it was with Abraham. And that is how it is with us. The Galatians, strongly rebuked by Paul for their attachment to the Jewish ceremonies and legalism associated with the Old Covenant, are nevertheless reminded that they are all Abraham's sons once they belong to Christ, whether they came from Jewish or Gentile stock. 'If you are Christ's, then you are Abraham's offspring, heirs according to promise' (Gal. 3:29). A little earlier in that chapter Paul had made a crucial distinction between the covenant linking God's grace and Abraham's response (which the law could not annul) and the Old Testament law itself (given to Moses 430 years afterwards and treated by many Jews as a claim on God, almost a means of twisting his arm). Lawkeeping cannot establish any claim on God, Paul maintains. Why, then, was it given? 'It was added because of transgressions until the offspring should come to whom the promise had been made' (3:19). Two reasons, you note. One is to show sin up as the heinous thing it really is. And the second is to be a provisional enactment until Christ should come, when it would become obsolete. And so it proved. The law's restriction of grace to one nation, the Jews, became obsolete. The special food laws became obsolete. It was in this sense, as the writer to the Hebrews saw, that 'In speaking of the new covenant he treats the first as obsolete. And what is becoming obsolete and growing old is ready to vanish away' (Heb. 8:13).

That was very true when the Epistle to the Hebrews was written. The old Jewish observances, to which some of his readers were so attached, were indeed obsolete, and were about to be proved so, in the sovereign purposes of God, by the destruction of Jerusalem in AD 70. But the covenant of grace with faith is not obsolete. That was not discontinued. It was the supreme covenant of God, running through from Abraham's day to our own. And it was 'new' in the sense that it makes Christ more explicit, enables us to understand what 'blood' takes away sins, embraces men and women of every race, puts the Holy Spirit (long hoped for by Jeremiah and Ezekiel) into every believing heart. Yes, in these and other senses the New Covenant is indeed not only new but everlasting. Nothing needs to be added to it (as there did to the Old Covenant, which was still looking forward to the coming of Christ and the free availability of his Spirit). But it is *not* new in the sense that it is totally discontinuous with the Old. God has not changed his mind or his way of salvation. The very passages in Hebrews which my Baptist friend cites in favour of discontinuity point in precisely the opposite direction. The whole point of Hebrews 9 depends on the fact that the same word in Greek is used for 'covenant' and for 'will'. Now a will is not effective without the death of the testator. So it is with God's will or covenant. It did not reach its full effectiveness until the animal sacrifices of the old were replaced by the sacrifice of the Lord himself on Calvary. But it is one and the same covenant! This difference between the old and the new is not so much a matter of continuity and discontinuity. It is more a matter of promise and fulfilment in the age-long relationship of God to his people.

Romans 3.24–6 makes precisely the same point, though

it does not use the actual word 'covenant'. The work of Christ on Calvary availed not only prospectively but retrospectively 'to show God's righteousness in forbearing to punish former sins'. God dealt with the backlog on the cross as well as with the prospective future debts. And the next chapter makes great play of the fact that David and Abraham were saved and justified in precisely the same way as the (mainly) Gentile readers of Romans – because they trusted in the sheer grace of God. Two covenants; yes indeed. But only one way of salvation, whereby sinful man puts his trust in the God who, at enormous personal cost, acquits the ungodly.

The second stricture of my Baptist friend can be dealt with much more briefly. He complains that I do not take seriously the rise of individualism and the new spiritual qualifications required of the people of the new covenant. I must plead 'not guilty' to that! The stress in this book on the need for personal response is very clear. But 'the rise of individualism' can have a less healthy nuance about it. It can detract from the strongly biblical emphasis, in New Testament as well as Old, on the solidarity of the family and the church. We are not just individuals; but sometimes Baptist emphasis on individual and personal faith could lead us to suppose we were.

Of course, if *I* am right in seeing one single covenant of grace and faith running through the entire Bible, then *he* is right in his third stricture that sometimes the church has to embrace the unregenerate and the hypocrite. I fear it does. It did in the Old Covenant with an Ishmael and an Esau. It does in the New, with an Ananias and a Simon Magus. In this fallen world there is no possibility of having a completely 'pure' church. Not only is every member flawed and defiled, but there is no certain way of discerning the 'hypocrite' from the 'real'. We can only hear a person's profession, look at his life, and make a provisional assessment: it is God alone who can see into the heart. The search for the pure church this side of heaven is bound for disappointment. Charles Spurgeon is once reputed to have said to a woman who was seeking a 'pure' church: 'Don't look for a pure church, madam, for you will not find one. And if you do, be sure you do not join it, for you would only spoil it!' 'In the visible church,' according to the Thirty-nine Articles of Religion, 'the evil will ever be mingled with the good, and sometimes the evil have chief authority in the ministration of the Word and Sacraments' (Article 26).

'However defective the hypocrite's personal standing before God,' writes Bishop Colin Buchanan, 'his relation to the people of God is clear – he has been incorporated, and is reckoned with them from his baptism . . . He belongs. He is "one of us". We do not even know which of our Christian friends he is. There may be no such hypocrite among the Christians we know. We treat them all as Christians' (*A Case for Infant Baptism*, p. 17). Inevitably there may be counterfeit Christians as well as real ones in any church, just as in Israel long ago. One day, at Christ's return, he will pluck up the weeds from his corn. Meanwhile, said Jesus, 'Let both grow together until the harvest' (Matt. 13.30).

2. *'You rely too much on the dubious Old Testament argument from circumcision'*

My gentle Baptist critic put it well when he wrote, 'For an increasing number of Christians, taking norms from the Old Testament and willy-nilly building Christian teaching on them is suspect.' Fair enough, when the New Testament modifies the Old. But if the New Testament and Apostolic Fathers simply continue to operate as Christians in much the same way as the Old Testament laid down for Jews, maybe the good Lord intended no change!

But are there not insuperable differences between circumcision in the Old Covenant and baptism in the New? For one thing, circumcision was for boys only; baptism is for all. For another, circumcision was automatic for putting males into the covenant, whereas baptism is clearly not universally effective.

Let us deal with the second point first. You were *not* automatically made a member of the Old Covenant by your birth into Judaism followed by circumcision. Remember how Ishmael was circumcised as well as Isaac, but both were not automatically members of the covenant people of God. 'The son of this slave woman shall not be heir with my son Isaac' (Gen. 21:10). It was the same with Jacob and Esau. 'Two nations are in your womb . . . the elder shall serve the younger' (Gen. 25:23), and 'I have loved Jacob but I have hated Esau' (Mal. 1:2–3). Interestingly enough, Paul uses these very texts in his famous passage on rejection in Romans 9. There was nothing automatic about being a member of the Israel of God just because you were circumcised. 'He is not a real Jew who is one outwardly, nor is true circumcision something external and physical' (Rom. 2:28).

As for the first point, I am not arguing that circumcision is in all respects parallel to baptism. It is manifestly not – women were not circumcised, whereas they are baptised. I am simply saying that just as there was a physical mark to initiate the children of believers into the Old Covenant, so there is in the New. What was restricted to Jewish males under the Old Covenant is available to all under the New, female as well as male, Gentiles as well as Jews. St Paul brings baptism and circumcision together in a significant and closely-knit argument in Colossians 2:11, 12. It runs like this: 'In him also you were circumcised with a circumcision made without hands, by putting off the body of flesh in the circumcision of Christ; and you were buried with him in baptism, in which you were also raised with him . . . from the dead.' Paul is maintaining that the Old Testament practice of circumcision reached its fulfilment in the circumcision of Jesus. This was no partial and ritual setting aside of evil from the life by removing the foreskin; but rather a total and actual victory over evil itself through the cross. That was Christ's real circumcision, just as it was his real baptism. But far from teaching that the external mark of belonging was no longer important under the New Covenant, Jesus taught that it was. His disciples were to go out and baptise (Matt. 28:19). So it is very natural for Paul in this passage to draw together the covenant marks of circumcision and baptism and to relate them both to the supreme event from which they derive their meaning and their efficacy, the work of Jesus on the cross at the mid-point of redemption history. And from the earliest days this parallelism between the sign of the Old Covenant and of the New was recognised in the church. We find it not only here in Paul, but also in Justin Martyr. Writing in the middle of the second century he draws a clear parallel between baptism and circumcision (*Dialogue* 43).

I believe we can, therefore, place a good deal of weight on the link between baptism and circumcision. Neither automatically brings about what it signifies. Both are once and for all. Both admit the recipient into the fellowship of the people of God on this earth. Both call for a life of holiness. Both are the sign of the covenant. Both are the seal of the righteousness which comes by faith (Rom. 4:11). And if, despite the fact that infants could not believe, the sign of righteousness by faith was applied to them under the Old Covenant, and by divine decree at that (Gen. 17:9ff), why should it be denied to the children of believers under the New Covenant?

The argument from circumcision is strong.

3. *'Indiscriminate baptism of infants is a scandal'*

I agree. It is. There is no suggestion in the Old Testament
that circumcision should be for all and sundry: it should be
restricted to the children of the covenant. The same, by
parity of reasoning, should apply in the New Covenant, if
baptism is the counterpart of circumcision (just as the
Communion is the counterpart of Passover). Indiscriminate baptism tends to occur when you have a national
church; when, for example, all Englishmen think they have
a claim to be Church of England or all Serbians to be
Orthodox. It tends to surface when the church is at a low
ebb of holiness and evangelism, and when there is no
baptismal discipline. And it tends to be more prevalent
when those who practise it have an almost magical view of
the sacrament and see its effect as *ex opere operato* rather
than conditional on repentance and faith.

Baptists and members of the new charismatic communities frequently criticise the nominalism of the main-line
churches which baptise infants. They are right to do so. It is
often said that infant baptism lulls people into a state of
false security about their position before God. I fear it
does. But it need not. It should not lull the children of
believers into false security, and it is meant only for the
children of believers.

But if you agree that indiscriminate baptism of infants is a
scandal, and that the rite should only be reserved for
the children of believers, at once you run into another
problem. How are you to tell who is a real believer? By
regular church attendance? But are there no hypocrites
among regular attenders? Any baptismal discipline is
hard to operate, readily misunderstood, and full of
difficulties.

Even if it were possible to provide a workable discipline,
would that not be very unfair on other children? No, it
would not. God is just as willing to receive children from

non-Christian homes as he is from Christian homes. They are no worse off. It is ludicrous to suppose, as some churchmen have, that a child will go to hell if he dies unbaptised. What sort of a monster would act like that? Not the God portrayed to us in the Bible! Christ died not for our sins only but for the sins of the whole world (1 John 2:2). No, the unbaptised child is not disadvantaged: he simply lacks the mark of the covenant. That is all. His parents naturally cannot (and should not) desire for him what they will not accept for themselves. But that need not affect his destiny in this world or the next. He can come to a personal faith and then enjoy the privilege and joy of experiencing baptism as an adult. So far from being disadvantaged, he is arguably better off.

4. *'What are we to say of the millions who have the Christian sign but not the Christian reality?'*

Alas, that is all too possible. John the Baptist and Jesus himself were often attacking that sort of hypocrisy in those who sheltered under the umbrella of the covenant sign without committing themselves to the God who gave it. It was an ever-present danger under the Old Covenant, and it remains just as present under the New. But I see no reason why hypocrisy and false profession should rob children of the covenant from the badge of membership. After all, the prevalence of forged money does not turn us off the real thing! The words of Paul about circumcision quoted above, are just as applicable to baptism: 'He is not a real Jew who is one outwardly, nor is true circumcision something external and physical. He is a Jew who is one inwardly, and real circumcision is a matter of the heart' (Rom 2:28–9). Externalism has always been the foe of true religion. There have always been those 'having a form of god'iness but denying its power' (2 Tim. 3:5).

5. *'What good does it do to be baptised if you never come to Christ?'*

What, in that case, has your baptism effected? The answer must be 'nothing at all'. For baptism is like a cheque which may be said to convey to us a thousand pounds, but which does nothing of the sort if we do not cash it. So baptism is often spoken of in very realist language, as if it effected what it symbolised. But it does not effect our justification, new birth, and a life full of the Spirit *until and unless we cash the cheque*, and claim personally what has been made over to us in the purposes of the generous heavenly Father. So you are not 'saved' if you remain a baptised unbeliever. You are not a Christian. But you bear upon your body the mark of how much God the Father cares for you, of what Christ did for you, of what new birth in the Spirit could mean to you – if only you will trust him and obey.

6. *'Why baptise children if they cannot repent and believe?'*

The very way this difficulty is framed shows that the questioner has already decided what baptism means. He is already clear that it should be seen as the mark of our faith rather than of God's gracious initiative. Of course, the covenant sign is the mark *both* of God's grace *and* of our response: the problem is, which end of the stick to tie the sign to!

In point of fact, there is no text in the New Testament which says you must believe before you can be baptised. And if you tell me that Acts 8:37 is such a verse I will point out to you that the whole sentence, 'And Philip said "If you believe with all your heart, you may [sc. be baptised]"' is consigned to the margin by modern Bibles because it forms no part of the original Greek text.

But although there is no one text which says, 'You may not be baptised unless you are a believer', the association of repentance and faith with Christian baptism is so central that it cannot be swept aside just because the recipient is too young to understand. Nor is it, in any respectable service of infant baptism. The Christian family and the Christian church gather round the infant. The parents express their own repentance and faith, and this is the warrant for proceeding to baptise the child. But that act cannot take place until the child speaks through its godparents, and expresses (in germinal form) that repentance and faith which are the human conditions of the new birth.

This may seem very odd, but is it? It takes seriously the fact that children were part of the New Testament church. They belonged. And there are numerous injunctions given specifically to them in the letters of the New Testament (e.g. Eph. 6:1–3; Col. 3:20; 1 John 2:12–14). They are addressed as being 'in the Lord', and this phrase must make it more than probable that they were baptised. He is their Lord as well as their parents' Lord. They are not released from the obligations imposed by baptism: they are expected to repent and believe, in ways appropriate to their age, and they are brought up in a climate where this is in fact the way of life. So they learn to say 'sorry', not only to their parents but to God from the earliest days. They learn to trust a mother as they hang on her breast – a mother, moreover, who herself refuses to play God to the child, but realises and confesses her own sinfulness and her own dependence upon the Lord. There is therefore nothing at all artificial about the idea of the child speaking through its sponsors. It is not only a regular legal device, but it is in fact the way in which little people do develop in a home. They learn from the climate about them. And if that is one of repentance and faith, in which Christ is honoured as Lord, then there is every reason to expect that they will exhibit the same qualities. Just as there is no known moment in

the natural life of a child when consciousness starts, so it is
with many in their spiritual lives. They have never known a
time when they did not trust and obey the Lord who is
worshipped by their parents and comes at his own initiative
in baptism to offer them the precious gifts of new birth,
membership of his family, pardon for sin, and the indwelling of the Holy Spirit. Was it not Luther who said, 'A child
has the same faith as you or I when we are asleep'?

Hard though it may be for us rationalistic Westerners to
understand the notion of repentance and faith by a child
through its proxy, the godparent, it is not at all hard to
understand that in baptism Christ holds out to us his grace
in all its fullness. And baptism is the pledge of that divine
initiative, even more than of our responsive faith. It marks
upon the child all that Christ achieved for him by his
coming, his dying and his rising. To be sure, the child will
need to show that he has responded to this gracious initiative. Without response, the death of Christ for him will do
him no good. But in bringing their children to baptism
Christians express the confidence that, given the right
upbringing in the home and worship in the church, the child
will not be such a fool as to turn down these marvellous gifts
the Lord is holding out to him. That was the attitude of faith
and hope in which Jews brought their children to circumcision, and it is eminently appropriate for Christians
bringing their children to baptism.

7. *'Why do liturgies such as the Anglican speak of the
baptised child as "born again" and "an inheritor
of the kingdom of heaven"?'*

Is this not arrant fantasy? Yes, if you look at it from one
point of view. No, if you look at it from another. If you take
'regenerate', 'born again', 'inheritor of the kingdom of
heaven' and suchlike language out of context then it *is*

arrant nonsense, and I would not defend it for a moment. But this is *liturgical* language. And liturgies must be based on the supposition that people mean what they say. The child is said to repent (through its sponsors); it is said to believe; and consequently it is said to be born again. It is no more literally born again than it literally repents and believes. This is all the language of faith, of covenant, and it must be taken as such.

Only so can you understand many of the prayers of the church. Take, for example, the collect for Sexagesima Sunday, 'O God, who seest that we put not our trust in anything that we do . . .' Is that claim literally true for all members of the church? Or when the Burial Service speaks of 'our dear brother here departed', *was* he a Christian brother? You have to interpret all liturgies in the spirit of formal supposition, assuming that the inner reality accords with the language of faith. The Anglican Church certainly does not believe that all baptised children are 'regenerate' in the full sense of 'spiritually reborn'. The sign is not the same as the thing signified. The Thirty-nine Articles of Religion make short work of any automatic view of sacramental grace. It is, says Article 25, 'in such only as worthily receive' the sacraments of baptism and Communion that 'they have a wholesome effect or operation'. It is only, Article 27 asserts, those who 'receive baptism *rightly*' that are 'grafted into the Church'. What is meant by *rightly* is made clear in the 26th Article, which speaks of 'such as *by faith and rightly* do receive the sacraments'. I make no apology for going back to the old Prayer Book and the Thirty-nine Articles. These are the historic formularies of the Anglican Church, one of the ancient Churches of Catholic Christendom which was reformed by the standard of Scripture in the sixteenth century. The Baptism Service of the Anglican Church (which declares children 'regenerate') was framed by Martin Bucer, a continental Reformer, who was a friend of Archbishop Cranmer and who certainly did not believe in any automatic rebirth of the baptised, be they adult or infant. There had to be repentance and faith. Cranmer agreed. 'All that be washed in water be not washed with the Holy Spirit,' he said. And looking around you, that is very obvious! Perhaps Archbishop Ussher hit the nail on the head when he wrote,

> As baptism administered to adults is not effectual unless they believe, so we can make no comfortable use of our baptism as infants until we believe. All the promises of grace were estated upon me in baptism, and sealed up to me on God's part: but I come to have the profit and benefit of them when I come to understand what God in baptism has sealed to me, and actually lay hold on it by faith.

More than a thousand years beforehand Augustine had said something very similar. 'Outward baptism may be administered where inward conversion of the heart is wanting: and, on the other hand, inward conversion of the heart may exist where outward baptism has never been received.'

It is essential that we distinguish between the potential and the actual, between the sign and the thing signified, in all liturgical language. Failure to do this has been disastrous, and nowhere is it more dangerous to neglect this distinction than in the sacraments of baptism and the eucharist. Each has an outer form and an inner reality. These are not necessarily identical. As one wise archbishop put it long ago, 'Some have the outward sign, and not the inward grace. Some have the inward grace, but not the outward sign. We must not commit idolatry by deifying the outward element.'

With this in mind, we can return to the baptismal liturgies with their realistic language about the rebirth of the infant candidates. Strange though it looks at first sight, there is a profound logic in this sort of language. To the eye of faith the child is seen as speaking through its godparents, repenting of its sins and trusting in Christ. Only after that is the consequence of such an attitude expressed: any person who repents and believes is indeed born again and becomes an inheritor of the kingdom of heaven. And the rite of baptism marks him out as such. Whether that child will be what he professes remains to be seen. The liturgies of the church give him a marvellous opportunity to make these things his own in the public rite of confirmation, where he reiterates the promises made for him as a child and expresses his personal commitment to Christ.

The point is that *no liturgy can create reality*. A person may go through not only infant baptism but adult baptism or confirmation without a whiff of reality. I know, because I did it. So the promises of God made in baptism and reiterated at confirmation remain the language of promise, of potentiality, until the time when the person claims them for himself. I thank God for that day in my own life. There was nothing wrong with the promises of God, nor with the liturgy I had been through. It was simply that I had never understood nor fulfilled the conditions of repentance and faith that were required, and therefore I was not yet that regenerate participant in the Holy Spirit which, on the principles of faith, hope and charitable supposition, the liturgy had asserted me to be.

8. *'But there was no faith around at my baptism!'*

People who come to see the conditional language of the Prayer Book, and that it makes sense to talk like that within the community of faith, are often concerned about this matter. They see no sign of living faith in their parents. The church where they were baptised seems dead. With the charm of youth they wonder if the minister was ever converted. What was such an infant baptism worth?

The 26th Article of the Church of England has a good answer to that problem. It speaks of the unworthiness of the minister not hindering the grace of the sacrament. It says, 'Neither is the effect of Christ's ordinance taken away by their wickedness or the grace of God's gifts diminished from such as by faith and rightly receive the sacraments.' Do you trust the Lord now? Are you in the right with him now? Then you can be sure that the sacrament was valid. Baptism is a sacrament of the grace of God to sinners. We are not invited to hold an enquiry into the supposed spiritual state of those who brought us to the sacrament! The church is the household of faith, however wobbly some of its members are. And you were brought within that household for baptism. You have subsequently come to faith and are yourself a member of that household. You received the mark of belonging then. You believe now. Take heart. The outer sign and the inner reality have come to correspond in your life.

In any case, just think what a chaotic situation would ensue if we had to be assured that a particular amount of faith had to be present at a baptism before it could be reckoned a baptism! How much faith? Who has to have it? What if it was not quite enough? Or theologically deficient? The faith of parents and sponsors bringing a child to baptism is very important when the church is considering who are fit subjects for baptism. But once the decision to baptise a particular child has been taken, then you simply can't attempt to assess the validity of the sacrament by holding an inquisition into the amount of faith present. With the value of hindsight one may even come to the conclusion that it would have been better had the child not been baptised. But baptised it was, and nothing can change that. One of the main strands in baptism is to give us an objective assurance about what God has done for us; it is not to plague us with doubts as to whether we are worthy enough or have fulfilled the right conditions. Baptism, like the grace of God which it embodies, is essentially for the *unworthy!*

9. *'Infant baptism is so often an empty ceremonial, a hole-in-the-corner affair'*

It is administered with a token sprinkling of water, without instruction of the parents and godparents, without preaching, and in the middle of the afternoon when nobody else is there. 'We want it nice and private, Vicar!'

Alas, all of that is true in some places at some times. It is totally indefensible. The mark of entry into the covenant should be a time of celebration, of public welcome into Christ's body, the church. It should take place after careful instruction of the parents and godparents beforehand, and of the congregation at the occasion itself. Many of the main-line churches have been appallingly lax over this, and have only themselves to blame for the nominalism and superstition which have come to surround this sacrament in the minds of many. What is the good of a white robe and Jordan water, if there is no reality on the part of those closely concerned?

Baptism should take place in the body of the congregation at one of the main services. This holds good whether we are talking about infant or adult baptism, whether it is held in the church or beside the river. It is a public declaration of repentance, faith, the grace of God, the coming of the kingdom and the welcome of the church. It is not, and it cannot be right to make it, a hole-in-the-corner affair.

Equally, there must be instruction of the parents and godparents. The whole principle of infant baptism presupposes reality of faith in those who bring the child. How can they bring the infant up as a Christian, how can they make Christian things real to him if these things are not real to them? How can they want for their child what they have not received for themselves? Infant baptism is a marvellous opportunity not only to face the parents and godparents with their duties in bringing up the child, but also to challenge them about their own relationship with God. Do they want to be hypocrites, claiming publicly in the service on behalf of the child that repentance, faith and obedience which they know is not true in their own lives? I do not think the minister should peer into the hearts of parents and godparents. It is, mercifully, God's job to do that – not the minister's. But it is his job to show them the importance of the vows they are taking and the danger of hypocrisy if they do not really mean them. And I believe a minister would be totally within his rights not only in requiring regular church attendance from those applying for the baptism of their children, but also in refusing to baptise the next child if the family had ceased to come to church subsequent to the baptism of the first one. We must not conduct an inquisition into the motives of those who make some profession of the Christian faith: but we must require firm profession and some evidence of its reality before we baptise young children.

Need for reform

We have glanced in this chapter at nine objections either to infant baptism as such, or else as it is widely practised. They add up to a formidable list. They show that baptismal discipline has been terribly lax, and baptism teaching deplorably weak. They make it very easy to understand the Baptist protest, and to sympathise with it. I cannot deny the propriety of infant baptism, for the reasons advanced in the last chapter. But I can appreciate that its indiscriminate use has led millions to assume blandly that they are Christians when they are not. I would even be willing, in recognition

of the failures in our paedobaptist churches, to give up
infant baptism for one generation if that were possible! It
would clear the ground, and enable us to have a fresh start,
with the sign of the covenant marking out believers and
their children. For this is the only sort of infant baptism
which can be justified from Scripture, or, for that matter,
from the formularies of the Church of England. Of course,
it is not possible to put the clock back and start again. In any
case abuse does not take away proper use. But it should
make paedobaptist churches look very carefully to their
practice if they are not to perpetuate the scandal of indiscriminate baptism which has brought the whole principle of
infant baptism into such disrepute in many thoughtful
Christian circles. If infant baptism is practised, it must lead
on to discipleship. In liturgical terms, it must issue in the
personal commitment of confirmation, and that is the
subject of our next chapter.

7
BAPTISM AND CONFIRMATION

The status of confirmation

In the early days of the church baptismal ritual was varied, and sometimes very evocative. Often, the candidate after confession of sin and profession of faith would go down into the water of the river or baptistry and be totally immersed, three times, in the name of the Father, the Son and the Holy Spirit. He would emerge the other side, and then three actions would follow. He would be clothed in a white garment, as a picture of the perfect new standing that was his in Christ. He would be given some milk and honey to eat, an emblem of the Promised Land after the passage through the Red Sea. And hands would be laid upon him to express his incorporation into the Christian community and their solidarity with him.

This was fine for the adult believer, but some modification was clearly required for the child. Some of the imagery was dropped, and before long the laying on of hands was reserved for a later time when the youngster was old enough to reiterate the promises and the expression of faith made on his behalf when he was baptised.

There is no ground in Scripture for this 'confirmation', unless it be in the tantalising allusion in Hebrews 6:1. 'Therefore let us leave the elementary doctrine of Christ and go on to maturity, not laying again a foundation of repentance from dead works . . . with instruction about ablutions, the laying on of hands, the resurrection of the dead, and eternal judgment.' No, confirmation is not a biblical rite: it is simply a practice of the ancient church in the West since the third century, and accordingly it has become a domestic requirement of some Churches, among them the Church of England. There is a lot to be said for such a rite if you stay with infant baptism. For although confirmation as such is not to be found in Scripture, the reaffirmation of vows made for you as a child most certainly is. Just as the Jew, circumcised on the eighth day, had to take upon himself 'the yoke of the Law' in the bar mitzvah ceremony at about the age of 12, so those baptised in infancy need to have an opportunity to take their personal stand for Christ, and make their own what has been confidently hoped and prayed for on their behalf at their baptism. Confirmation provides just this.

What confirmation is not

First of all, it may be helpful to clear what is sometimes, to judge from the sermons of bishops conducting confirmations, something of a jungle.

Confirmation is not the topping up of baptism as the entry into the Christian life. There is no justification for such a view anywhere in the New Testament. It is no supplementary rite. Repentance, faith and baptism are the human conditions for receiving the new life in Christ, membership of his family, the forgiveness of sins and the gift of his Spirit. Baptism alone is the rite which initiates a person into the church; not baptism and something else, i.e. confirmation. This is now widely recognised, in reaction against the theory of two-stage initiation which dominated Anglicanism earlier this century, led by men like Couratin, Dix and Fisher. The earliest post-apostolic description of Christian initiation, in Justin Martyr in the middle of the second century, knows nothing of confirmation. The candidates were baptised outside the church and then brought into the service, which was presided over by the bishop, and were greeted with the kiss of peace and shared in the Communion. No sniff of confirmation! It was just the same in the Eastern Church. Neither the *Didache* nor Ignatius know anything about it. They are clear that baptism and baptism alone is the rite of Christian initiation. Properly, therefore, the Church of England's *Ely Report on Initiation* (1971) stated 'Baptism cannot be added to or supplemented or "completed". It is the one and complete sacrament of Christian initiation.' Confirmation merely gives the candidate the opportunity to make more explicit and personal one strand in baptism, the confessional strand, which had been impossible in infancy.

Equally, there is no scriptural justification for the notion that the person coming to confirmation receives the gift of the Holy Spirit then and there for the first time. Yet to hear some bishops, you would think that in confirming they were the unique agency through whom the Spirit of God came upon the candidates. The proposed 1928 Prayer Book, which in its wisdom Parliament rejected because the Church of England was so divided about it, had a lection for confirmation which lent colour to this view. The passage was Acts 8, where, through the agency of the apostles who came down from Jerusalem, the gift of the Holy Spirit came upon Samaritans who had previously been baptised. Indeed, the 1928 Confirmation Service goes so far as to say 'The Scripture here teacheth us that a special gift of the Holy Spirit is bestowed through the laying on of hands with prayer.'

But it is by no means evident that Acts 8 can be taken as a precedent for so broad a claim. It is a unique and much disputed passage, and it is as well to remember, before building a doctrine of initiation through confirmation upon it, that this is precisely the pillar passage to which Pentecostals turn in order to justify their version of two-stage initiation. Both can't be right. Probably neither is. For Acts 8 is an exceptional situation, whatever view of baptism, confirmation and the Holy Spirit you take. It stands quite on its own and it cannot bear the weight thrust upon it by claims for two-stage initiation made either by Catholic or Pentecostal theologies. For a fuller examination of that passage, see my *I Believe in the Holy Spirit*, Chapter 8.

At all events, no such exaggerated claims were made in the Book of Common Prayer which saw the laying on of hands by the bishop in confirmation not as some magical rite to impart the (previously absent) Holy Spirit to the candidate, but rather 'to certify them by this sign of thy favour and gracious goodness towards them. Let thy fatherly hand, we beseech thee, ever be over them. Let thy Holy Spirit ever be with them.' And that is a very different matter. Not supplementary initiation, but a symbolic act of prayerful confirming, or strengthening those who confirm their vows of repentance, faith and obedience. And it is the Book of Common Prayer, not the utterances of confirming bishops, which indicates the teaching of the Anglican Church.

If confirmation is neither a supplementary rite of initiation, nor a means for imparting the Holy Spirit to those previously devoid of him, what is it?

What confirmation is

It is, first and foremost, a profession of faith. The one element in baptism which is denied the infant is that of confession. He cannot respond to the grace of God which approaches him in the sacrament of baptism. He needs an opportunity to make public profession of his own personal surrender to the Lord, his own profession of repentance and faith. Confirmation gives him this opportunity. There are basically two parts to it. He confirms the vows and the faith expressed for him by his godparents as a child. And the bishop lays his hands upon the candidate to assure him by this sign that God can be relied upon to confirm and strengthen him in the Christian life to which he has openly committed himself. So there are two confirmations, not one. The candidate confirms his Christian profession. The Lord confirms his protection and strength for the battle ahead.

Confirmation is, second, a domestic rite bringing the candidate into full accreditation and recognition within a particular branch of the Christian church. Baptism is *never* denominationally orientated. A person is baptised not into the Methodists or the Anglicans but *into Christ* and his worldwide church. But confirmation, or its equivalent, is used by some churches of a divided Christendom to bring a person into full standing within a particular denomination. In baptism I was made a member of Christ and of his one, holy, catholic, apostolic church. In confirmation, I was brought into full communicant and voting standing within the Church of England. For confirmation is no supplementary rite to Christian baptism. It is a domestic ordinance for determining enfranchisement within one part of the universal church, in my case the Anglican.

Third, confirmation is a commissioning for service. It contains a prayer that the candidate may continue Christ's for ever, and daily increase in his Holy Spirit. It is a commissioning service; not, as many seem to take it, a passing-out parade.

The problems of admission to Communion

Of course, whenever you create an extra-biblical intermediate rite, such as confirmation, you run into problems. One of them is the question of Holy Communion.

Should the criterion of receiving Communion in, say, the Church of England be confirmed membership of that Church (or one of its sister Churches)? Or should all baptised believers in Christ be invited to its celebrations of the Holy Communion? A few decades ago it was customary to insist on episcopal confirmation as a precondition of Communion. Now that is recognised as historically and theologically misguided and is largely defunct. The new canon laws of the Church of England allow baptised members of any church, if they are in good standing with their own denomination, to share the Communion in Anglican churches. The expectation is, of course, that if they propose to do this regularly they will change their denomination, and become confirmed members of the Anglican Church.

This lowering of the barriers is healthy, and brings us nearer to the attitudes of the New Testament Church, which resolutely refused the temptation to form a number of different denominations. How easy it would have been to have a Jewish Church, a Samaritan Church, and a Gentile Church within the first decade of the new movement! This they resisted, in the name of one God, one faith, one baptism. Jesus prayed that Christians should be one, identifiably belonging to one another; and nothing less should be our goal. However disappointing the ecumenical movement may sometimes seem, it is groping towards an ideal for which all Christians should strive, and especially those who value Scripture highly. Alas, these are often the least interested in ecumenism.

Good though this increasing openness to other Christians is, it brings problems in its wake. For the Book of Common Prayer insisted on confirmation by the bishop before people received the Holy Communion. It can be shown that this was a domestic ordinance of the Church of England for her own members, and that the present exercise of eucharistic hospitality is merely an extension of what had been Anglican practice since the Reformation to a greater or lesser extent. But the current effect of loosening the restrictions, and inviting all baptised Christians to the Lord's table, is that many young people, converted through the Anglican Church, are by no means itching for confirmation within that Church.

We find that among Oxford undergraduates at St Aldate's. Large numbers of students, many of whom come up to the university as agnostics, are brought to Christian faith each year. They are nurtured and, of course, baptised if they have not been baptised before. These baptisms are great occasions. They may be administered in church by pouring water on the candidate (affusion); or else down at the river by submerging the candidate (immersion). But by no means all these young people want to become confirmed members of the Anglican Church. They are aware of the deadness and formalism which pervades many areas of Anglicanism. They have come alive in Christ, and propose to look for a living body of believers with whom to throw in their lot when they leave university. Whether it is Anglican or not is of little importance to them. They see themselves as Christians first, Protestants second, and Anglicans third. Denominations are less and less significant to young people coming into faith these days.

This tendency is certainly not confined to Oxford. I have noticed, for example, in Canada, that the farther west you move the less influential the main-line denominations become, and the more dynamic is the growth of the newer charismatic, non-denominational churches. This trend may not commend itself to the leadership of the main-line churches, but it is a fact of life which has to be reckoned with. And it is accentuated by two factors at least. One is the voice of the community churches saying, 'Come out from among them and join us: we are restoring the purity of the primitive New Testament church.' That is attractive to many, even though the House Church Movement is now showing every sign of becoming just one more denomination, like most renewal movements down the course of history. But the other factor is the admission to Communion of new believers after conversion and baptism without the necessity of waiting for confirmation.

The issue of child participation in Communion

Another of the questions that is currently vexing many of the main-line churches which practise infant baptism, is whether or not the baptised children of Christian families should be entitled to receive Holy Communion. The normal practice is that they do not. The teaching of the Anglican Prayer Book is that they should not. The rubric following the Confirmation Service states it boldly. 'There shall none be admitted to the Holy Communion until such time as he be confirmed, or be ready and desirous to be confirmed.' The reason for this position is plain. It is to ensure that children know what they are doing when they come to the central mystery of the Christian faith. They must, as the 1662 Infant Baptism service puts it, be able to 'say the Creed, the Lord's Prayer and the Ten Commandments in the vulgar tongue, and be further instructed in the Church Catechism' which was set out in every copy of the Prayer Book. Accordingly, it has become customary for children to offer themselves for confirmation at any time between 7 and 16.

But there is an increasing dissatisfaction with this approach. Pastorally it is notably unsuccessful. There is an enormous fall-away rate among youngsters confirmed at this sort of age. It is psychologically unsatisfactory, too. The normal age of administering confirmation runs into all the confusions and changes of puberty, when the whole personality is in flux, and is arguably the very worst possible time to take any major decisions which may affect the whole of your future religious life. There are social snags, too. The child who is not allowed to partake in the Holy Communion with its parents can be made to feel a second-class citizen in the life of the church, and isolated from his parents. More important, he is denied the strength afforded by the sacrament just when he needs it so badly during the 'slippery paths of youth' and the turbulent age of adolescence. But the theological issue is paramount. Is baptism, or is it not, the sacrament of Christian initiation? If it is, then it does not need any rite to top it up. If it is not, then presumably confirmation ought to be urged on all other Churches as a vital gospel element which they had failed to notice! But as we have seen, there is no clear evidence for confirmation in the New Testament. It is a domestic ordinance for some Churches, and not more than that. Baptism is unambiguously the sacrament of entry into the church, and we must stick with that. Baptists have sometimes pointed (with good reason) to the inconsistency of Anglicans who claim that baptism is the rite of entry into the church and then behave as if confirmation really was! Their criticism is just. I believe we must grasp the nettle firmly and maintain both that baptism is the rite of entry and that children who have been baptised may take their share in the Holy Communion with their parents. This does not mean that confirmation is useless. Indeed, such a change could make it more useful than it is. For confirmation could then be postponed to late teens or early twenties when a young person has been able to think out his or her own attitudes to matters of Christian belief and belonging which they could not possibly do at the age of 14 or younger. This has been advocated by more than one Commission of the Church. It is, I believe, sure to come.

The point of confirmation after adult baptism

A growing trend in our society, which has for nearly a century been steadily moving away from the church, is adult baptism (and adult confirmation) as people are brought to faith. It is most satisfactory when the whole initiatory rite can take place all at once, and adult baptism be followed by confirmation and Communion. It was thus in the early church, when Easter was the great time for Christian initiation. But if some considerable time exists between adult baptism and confirmation, how is the person to regard himself? The answer must surely be that he is a full member of Christ and his universal church, but that he is not yet legally enfranchised within the Church of England, because he has not yet been through its domestic ordinance of confirmation.

It is much the same for a member of some other denomination, worshipping for the time being in an Anglican Church. If he wants to throw in his lot with the Anglicans, he must be confirmed. This need not be regarded as in any way a demeaning step, as if he needs to be made 'kosher'. All societies have their domestic arrangements for those wishing to join them, and churches are no exception. Confirmation for a mature, baptised adult Christian is neither rectifying some imagined inadequacy in such a person's Christian life, nor is it to be construed as a vote of no confidence in his previous denominational allegiance. It is simply a matter of getting into fellowship with the bishop, the local representative of the worldwide church of which the Anglican Communion is part.

Two important elements

Confirmation, therefore, should not be regarded as a matter of crucial importance. It does not bring a person into the church of God. That has been done, liturgically, in baptism. But it does mark him as belonging to a particular denomination: and in a fallen world with the one, holy, catholic and apostolic church split into various denominations, it is unfortunately necessary to bed down in one of them and settle into regular membership. Confirmation is how Anglicans, and some other Churches, bring this about. From confirmation onwards there is no question about full membership of the Anglican Church, with its responsibilities and privileges. And that is one aspect of confirmation which is not unimportant.

The other is much more significant. Somebody baptised as an infant has not had the opportunity for public and personal confession of his commitment to Christ. He needs that. It is an integral part of Christian initiation. 'If you confess with your lips that Jesus is Lord and believe in your heart that God raised him from the dead, you will be saved. For man believes with his heart and so is justified, and he confesses with his lips and so is saved' (Rom. 10:9–10). Yes, public confession of faith is an integral part of Christian belonging. Confirmation is the way some Churches make liturgical provision for this. It is an appropriate domestic ordinance for those baptised in infancy (or joining the Church from some other denomination) publicly to express their allegiance to Christ and to that particular branch of his church.

8
'REBAPTISM'

A surprising number of people these days ask for 'rebaptism'. Surprising, because it used not to be so. And surprising, too, because baptism is the sacrament of entry into the Christian life, and it is hard to see how you can have an entry a second time. Press them a bit, and they will admit this. But they will still want 'rebaptism' because in their view their first baptism wasn't any good. Now they want the real thing!

Why Do People Want 'Rebaptism'?

There are various reasons. But all of them see the first baptism, be it as an infant or, sometimes, as an adult, to be defective.

1. *For some, it is because there was not enough faith*

The most common approach comes from those who have come to an experience of evangelical conversion, and look back with suspicion on their baptism as infants. They didn't believe anything then. They were incapable of it. Moreover they are not at all sure that anyone else involved in the baptism believed much, either. There seems to have been a distinct shortage of faith. And clearly faith is necessary for baptism. Therefore the first baptism as an infant was no use. They want to disown it, and to have a proper believer's baptism.

But this really will not do. On this reasoning the Jew could doubt if his circumcision was valid. On this basis a man might doubt the validity of his marriage if he falls enthusiastically in love with someone else! A baptism is a baptism. It is administered with water into the name of the Father, the Son and the Holy Spirit. If my baptism was not valid because I did not believe enough, or not enough at the time, how could I ever be sure that I had been baptised? Baptism, the mark of belonging, the badge of assurance, would itself be worm-eaten with doubts. Nowhere in the New Testament is baptism seen as a witness to faith. That is sheer moonshine, despite being often repeated! To be sure, adults are not baptised unless and until they profess repentance and faith, but that does not mean that baptism is a witness to faith. It is nothing of the sort. It is a witness to the grace of God approaching me, embracing me, uniting me with Christ, and making me a member of his kingdom. Repentance and faith are not the gifts to which baptism bears witness: they are just the hands with which we grasp the gift.

2. *For some, it is because there was not enough confession*

There was no opportunity at their baptisms as infants (or conceivably at their baptisms earlier in their adult life) to bear witness to Christ, as they would now wish. The confessional element was lacking. But here again there is confused thinking.

For one thing, there was most certainly a confessional element in that earlier baptism, even if it was as an infant.

The church itself bore witness, through the presence of the congregation. The minister bore witness, by taking the service. The parents and godparents bore witness, by bringing the child in the first place, and by making public profession of the faith in which they brought him to be baptised.

For another thing, though, the baptism of infants looks beyond itself to public confession by the candidate when he is old enough to know what he is doing. The liturgical setting for this to take place is confirmation. And because confirmation seems often to be something of a 'sausage machine', something which is 'done' in middle and upper-class circles when teenage years arrive, the greatest care should be taken to give proper instruction. Those preparing the candidates should do their utmost to show that the service is robbed of all meaning if the candidate does not in fact repent, believe and turn to Christ. But if he does, or if he already has, then it is a marvellous opportunity to shout from the housetops that Jesus is Lord and that he is determined to follow him to the end.

In the church where I have been working, we ensure that every candidate for confirmation gives public testimony in his own words as to why he is there: either verbally in the service, or, if there are too many of them, in writing in the news-sheet. There is ample opportunity for the confessional element in initiation to be given full rein.

But sometimes people will come seeking 'rebaptism' because they were not converted at the time of their confirmation. They have therefore been robbed of the liturgical opportunity to bear public testimony to the grace of God which, by now, they have received. Great. That sort of thing happens. It happened to me. But what such people need is not a fresh baptism, but an opportunity to renew their baptismal vows publicly in the face of the congregation, and to give informal testimony as well. In baptism followed by confirmation you have the fullest possible expression of Christian initiation that liturgy can devise. When you have come, however belatedly, to appropriate what it offers you don't need to go through it all over again. You need to thank God, bear public testimony to his grace, and start living a steady, committed and different Christian life.

3. *For some, it is because there was not enough water*

They have become persuaded, perhaps by the arguments of Baptist friends, that baptism is not valid unless it is carried out through immersion. They believe this accords best with the symbolism of dying and rising with Christ which is so prominent in Romans 6.

But surely this is very strange, too. If God intended baptism to be valid only when it is by immersion, why is no hint of such a thing given in the Scriptures? Some of the baptisms which we hear of in the New Testament would have been rather difficult to do by immersion. Three thousand on the day of Pentecost, for a start. Where in Jerusalem, a city notoriously short of water, would they have found anywhere to do that? How easy would it have been to immerse the Ethiopian eunuch in the middle of the desert where there is only one little spring on the whole of that road going down to Gaza? How easily could the Philippian gaoler have found deep enough water in his house (especially after an earthquake!) to allow for immersion? I find it, on the contrary, a very moving thought that this man was probably baptised in the very water with which he had cleansed the wounds of his erstwhile prisoners, Paul and Silas.

The idea that immersion is necessary needs to be exploded. It cannot be shown from Scripture nor from the history of the church, which has sometimes poured water on candidates and sometimes immersed them in it.

It is not the amount of water that makes a person a Christian!

It is sometimes argued that the 'burial' imagery of Romans 6 demands immersion. But this cannot be so. No mention is made there of the mode of baptism, only of its efficacy. The ideas of 'burial' and 'raising' do not immediately conjure up thoughts of a river, but of a death and an empty tomb! The Bible uses various images connected with baptism. It is a fire to ignite us; it is water to wash us; it is a grave to bury us; it is new birth to inaugurate our Christian life; it is putting off the clothes of our old life and putting on Christ. There are many images associated with baptism. And none of them tells us in what manner baptism should be administered. Bishop Buchanan makes this point strongly in *One Baptism Once*, p. 24:

The symbolism of death and resurrection is not more foundational in the New Testament than that of new birth, or incorporation or 'putting on Christ' or even washing. Even if it were foundational it would *still* leave the mode an open question. Christians need to get clear in their minds that biblical symbolism is not to be identified with dramatic enactment, even though there may be some points of resemblance between the symbol and that which it symbolizes. Thus the Lord's Supper cannot contain *dramatization* of Calvary. The symbolism derives from Jesus' attachment of meaning to particular elements and actions, and *not* from any ability of ours to do these actions in such a way as to suggest verisimilitude. So it is with baptism. Submersion may be appropriate and powerful, but it cannot be requisite.

For what it is worth, the Church of England leaves open the option either of pouring water (not 'sprinkling') on the candidate, or dipping him in water. The Book of Common

Prayer, in the services both for adults and for infants, bids the minister either to dip or to pour water upon the candidate. Actually, pouring seems to be a second best, designed for those who cannot bear immersion! 'Then, naming it after the godparents, if they shall certify him that the child may well endure it, he shall dip it in the water discreetly and warily . . . But if they certify that the child is weak, it shall suffice to pour water upon it . . .' The same options are there in the modern Alternative Services Book. So candidates need to have it made very plain to them that there is a choice for them in this matter, and that if they prefer the mode of immersion they may gladly have it.

Of course, many churches do not have permanent facilities for immersion. This need be no problem. Some of my friends use an inflatable raft and put water inside it, not outside! Some use a child's paddling pool, or a jacuzzi. You do not need a great deal of water to immerse somebody completely. But I prefer to take adults who desire immersion down to the river and immerse them there, just below the Oxford university boathouse! As you can imagine, we gather a crowd as we go down the towpath, and the service itself is triumphant and full of joy and singing as the candidates give testimony to God's grace, to their response, and then go down into the water. On one such occasion two of the bystanders were converted. On another an extra person jumped into the water alongside her sister and five others. The symbolism was so powerful that it brought her, a young doctor who had been considering Christian commitment for some time, over the edge into baptism and discipleship. I love making full use of the variety allowed in the mode of baptism, and I have not only baptised infants and adults at the same service, but used affusion and immersion on the same day!

4. For some, it was because there was not enough feeling

We live in a very existential age. The value of many courses of action is judged on whether or not it feels good. And that attitude has spilled over to Christians. People hear of friends who have been baptised, and it made them feel so happy. Or they hear of the marvellous feelings as the waters close over your head. So they want it, too. They come to ask for a second baptism primarily in order to catch up on feelings.

Feelings come into it another way. When the minister asks a candidate for 'rebaptism' why he wants to come forward, the answer often is that he feels led, he has an inner urge, and so forth. Feelings again! If our Christian life depended on our feelings we should be in a real mess. Facts, faith, feelings should be kept strictly in that order. We should be as suspicious of getting 'rebaptised' because it feels good, as of getting remarried because it feels attractive. The Christian life is not meant to be a succession of kicks. We follow a crucified Messiah.

Baptism is all about entering the Christian life. It is not about feelings. It is a matter of dying and rising with Christ, not feeling good about him. It offers an unrepeatable new life, not an ephemeral new feeling. We need to distinguish very clearly between the two.

This cult of religious feelings is quite harmful to true Christian discipleship. For one thing it is so subjective: it tends to ignore the objectivity of the gospel, and make it, and baptism its symbol, a means for our own gratification. For another, it removes the necessity from baptism: if it is something I can go for if it makes me feel good, or repeat even though the New Testament tells me not to, then it removes baptism from the arena of Christ's command and my obedience. It degenerates into, 'If it suits you, have some.' And third, this self-gratifying approach to baptism tends to evacuate it of its corporate nature. 'Baptism is my witness to my faith: it happens when I want it, and if I leave it out altogether that is my business.' A good deal of modern thinking, not least in Evangelical circles runs something like that, and it is sub-Christian. For baptism is a corporate event: it puts me in Christ and in the church, and it is not a private feelings-warming exercise which I go in for at the hands of the leaders of the Christian Union in a college bath, or of a near-by Baptist minister when I never intended to become a member of his church.

What Is Wrong With 'Rebaptism'?

We have already begun to see an answer to that question as we have looked at the various reasons which bring people to ask for it. But there is one basic and very simple answer. *'Rebaptism' is wrong because it cannot be done!*

As we have seen earlier, baptism is the initiation of the Christian person. It is his inclusion in the salvation history of God. It is his incorporation into the church, the Body of Christ. And it is his immersion in the passion, death and resurrection of Jesus. Baptism means beginning. And it cannot be done again. It is by definition impossible to have more than one rite of initiation. It is as foolish as to petition for English citizenship when you are already a citizen; to seek adoption when you are already adopted. *Baptism is ever to be remembered but never to be repeated.* It cannot be. A baptism is a baptism. And, as we saw earlier, it does things. 'Baptism now saves us,' says the New Testament. 'We were buried with Christ by baptism.' 'As many of you as were baptised into Christ have put on Christ.' 'You were born again by water and the Spirit.' There are many such verses in Scripture. Baptism is effective. But it is not unconditionally effective. The conditions are repentance and faith. When those have not been present the man does not need baptism all over again. He needs to repent and believe! That is where the Reformers were so wise. They did not rebaptise. They knew too much theology. But they did speak of 'improving on' their baptism, by which they meant making use of its promises which had lain fallow and unclaimed for years. They possessed their possessions. They claimed for themselves the salvation which baptism symbolised and which had already been made over to them in the purposes of God and in the liturgy of the church.

There is a very instructive example of this in Acts 8. The Samaritans had been baptised at the preaching of Philip. For some reason, and we are not told what, this baptism did not do them any good. There was no evidence of the Holy Spirit in their lives. Two of the apostles came to Samaria from Jerusalem. They laid hands on them and prayed for them, and the Spirit's work became visible in their lives. What they did not do was to rebaptise them. They could not repeat what had already been done. For there is one God, one faith, one baptism. Christian baptism is unrepeatable.

Very well, let us apply that to the applicant for 'rebaptism'. He may feel his infant baptism was something he did not understand: that does not invalidate it, any more than it did for the Philippian gaoler who presumably understood very little at the time he was baptised. Baptism is not a mark of our understanding but of the covenant between a gracious God and us.

He may feel that his infant baptism was not accompanied by faith. It is most important that every care be taken to see that parents of infants to be baptised are believers. But we cannot see into the heart, and measure faith. Fortunately, however, baptism is not given us to celebrate our faith, but God's grace. The faith may come afterwards: the grace long antedates it. The baptism has taken place, however mixed the motives and low the spirituality of those involved. The person *is baptised* and nothing can unbaptise him.

He may feel that his baptism as an infant did him no good. A person may feel the same about his adult baptism, but that does not alter the fact that it was a baptism. It is not to be repeated. What is needed is for the human response, which was missing or mouthed hypocritically at that baptism, to be made with loving response from the heart to the Lord who offered him in baptism all the fruits of his death and resurrection.

For a baptism is a definable and observable event. It happened or it did not happen. It is the rite of entry into the Christian church. And by definition rites of entry cannot be repeated, nor can they be retrospectively invalidated.

What Can We Offer Those Who Seek 'Rebaptism'?

First, we should offer warmth. All too often such a request is frozen off by sharp disapproval from the minister who has been asked for it. We should rather 'rejoice with those that do rejoice'. When a person comes and seeks *any* step forward in the Christian life it is a case for love and encouragement and joy. God is clearly at work in such a person. He may have got it a bit wrong, but his love for the Lord is being stirred, and will respond to encouragement.

Second, we should offer explanation. We should show him that the once-for-all-ness of baptism is just like the once-for-all-ness of justification. It is something which by its nature cannot be repeated. He may regret the circumstances in which he was baptised: the fact remains that baptised he was, and nothing can change it. But we need to go farther than this. Our explanation needs to be not only destructive to get rid of a wrong notion, but constructive to show him more clearly the teaching of the Bible.

'Remembering' baptism

And one of the great words in the Bible is remembrance, *anamnēsis*. It is a powerful word. It was what the Israelite did at every festival: he 'remembered' that he had been a slave in Egypt, and the Lord his God redeemed him. He 'remembered' his redemption at every Passover meal. And it was no mere mental recollection. It was a re-entering of the event. 'This the Almighty did for *me* when *I* came out of Egypt' is a phrase in the Passover liturgy. Hundreds of years later the worshipper enters into the reality of the event he is celebrating. It is an opportunity to recall the event, to recover its power, and to renew his vow of allegiance in response. It is in this sense that the Lord's Supper is a memorial (*anamnēsis*, 1 Cor. 11:24). Not the remembering of a long past event, but a chance to enter into its reality afresh, recover its power, and offer ourselves to Christ anew.

> In 'remembering' baptism we are entering (a little more each time) into what God has done in and for us in this sacrament, calling into the present the power of what, historically, happened in the past, deepening our understanding of what we could never fully understand at the time of our baptism as infants or as adults, and appropriating more and more the grace made available to us.

Those words were written to me from Botswana by a lady who was once a Baptist missionary in what was then the Congo; she has now become an Anglican nun! She continued,

> 'Remembering' not only taps a powerful source of spiritual energy as we increasingly appropriate what God did for us and is doing in us, but we ourselves are

re-membered. We who are broken and fragmented by
life's experiences are 'put together again', healed, knit
together and re-membered as we enter again into the
Passion whereby he who was broken for us gives us
health and wholeness.

Baptised herself as an adult, she goes on,

> If we really understood this 'remembrance' we should
> not feel any need for the repetition of baptism even if we
> cannot consciously recall the original event. Those who
> feel that they missed the opportunity for public witness to
> their faith because they were baptized as infants, could
> ask to renew their vows publicly, and prepare for the
> occasion as seriously as though it was the initial act. And
> we should be able to come away from such an act clothed
> in baptismal freshness.

Reaffirming baptism

So, we can offer warmth, we can offer explanation, and we
can also offer opportunity. I sometimes think that too much
is made of a once-for-all public testimony. Baptism is too
important to be left to once-for-all testimony. It needs to
get out far more often than that! I should want to encourage
someone to speak often about Christ to his unconverted
friends: that is a fitting outworking of baptismal testimony.
I should encourage him to take the opportunity to renew his
baptismal vows to the Lord whenever present at the baptism of somebody else. I would suggest that every day
he make a short act of remembrance, following the
practice of Martin Luther who said every day of his life
'*Baptizatus sum* – I have been baptised'; or with D.H. Law-
rence, 'I have been dipped again in God and am new created'.
But I would also (and I regularly do) make opportunity

for the person who has come to see me about 'rebaptism' to give public testimony in a main service to what God has done in his life. Normally this is what he really longs to do, and it suffices. But sometimes he goes away and gets rebaptised in a Baptist or Pentecostal Church. If that happens, it is important not to ostracise him, but to welcome him back into the fellowship in love. He has acted conscientiously, even though we may think his conscience ill-informed, and we need to show our continued confidence in him and pastoral care for him.

Re-enacting baptism?

Just possibly there may be a way through between re-affirmation of baptismal vows, which might be thought to offer too little, and 'rebaptism' which offers confusion. It is a provision for the use of water to remind the candidate of his baptism long ago. It runs all the danger of being confused with a baptism, but this can be avoided with the careful use of language. Apparently the Presbyterian Church of New Zealand has recently made such provision to meet the psychological needs of those asking for 'rebaptism', but without sacrificing the 'one baptism' of which the New Testament speaks. It runs like this:

Brothers and sisters in Jesus Christ, in former days, before you knew it, God called you and laid his hand upon you to be his. By your baptism you were integrated into the true Vine, who is Christ; incorporated into the Body of Christ; seen to be infant members of the household of faith; lambs of the Good Shepherd's fold, to be nurtured by his grace.

Now by God's good hand he has brought you here, personally to accept his grace and declare yourselves by the power of his Spirit to be his own in repentance, faith and service. From first to last this has been the work of God. He has reconciled us men to himself through Christ, and he has enlisted us in this service of reconciliation.

After affirmations of faith, the candidates come forward for the immersion, and the minister says either

As you were baptized in the name of the Father and of the Son and of the Holy Spirit, so now I confirm to you the cleansing, forgiveness, new life, and promised gift of God's Holy Spirit which are in his covenant

or

As into Jesus Christ you were baptized, so I pray God who began a good work in you, to bring it to completion at the day of Jesus Christ.

It is not only in the Presbyterian Church of New Zealand that the pressures for 'rebaptism' have brought about this response. A celebrated Roman Catholic theologian told me that he had himself accorded very similar treatment in response to the same request. To be sure there is nothing in Scripture or church tradition which justifies this, unless it be the High Catholic practice of *asperges*, where the congregation are sprinkled with water to recall their baptism. But it does accord with the biblical notion of 'remembering', of bringing the past vividly into the present and recapturing both its power and our response. As such it might be used in circumstances where nothing less would satisfy. And it would assuredly not break the once-for-allness of salvation and the baptism which is its seal.

9
BAPTISM IN THE HOLY SPIRIT

The seal of the Spirit

'Long after the rest of the congregation had left, I stayed on in the church. I was pouring out my heart to God. I was grieved at the poverty of my Christian experience, my inability to break long-standing habits, my dullness in prayer and disinterest in the Bible. There was no power in my life, and little joy. I had no desire to tell others about Christ. I was parched and dry, and I knew it.

'And then as I waited on God in silence something amazing happened. I felt the presence of Jesus so close that I could almost reach out my hand and touch him. I was enveloped in his love and warmth. I knew that my prayers had been heard. I found myself weeping with joy, and breaking out into words which my mind did not form, a sort of new language. I found it led me into an entirely new dimension of prayer and praise. Whereas before I could only pray for a few minutes, now I wanted to pray all the time. I found myself praising God in this new tongue when driving the car and doing the washing-up. In the days that followed I found that other things had changed dramatically. I began to get mental pictures, often of other people in strange situations. When I plucked up courage to tell them, it almost always seemed to hit the nail on the head and meet a need which they had, but of which I was totally unaware. Then I remembered an occasion when my mother was laid low with a back injury. Very tentatively, I asked her if she would like to have me pray for her, and to my amazement she said she would. I did, and I found that these strange words came tumbling out as I prayed. She was amazed at this, but even more amazed when she felt a warmth coming strongly from my hands as I laid them upon the affected area of her spine. When I had finished praying she sat up – gingerly at first, and then confidently. She got up, bent, tried her back in various positions, and said in a tone of wondering amazement, "It is all fine now. The pain has gone and I can move naturally. This is wonderful."'

Things like this have been happening to millions of people in recent years. Initiation into this remarkable experience of spiritual power and joy is frequently called Baptism in the Holy Spirit.

Hitherto in this book we have paid scant attention to the third great strand in Christendom, alongside the Catholic and Protestant: namely, the charismatic. We have not returned to examine the view of the third person we met during our walk down the street in the first chapter. We have ignored the Pentecostal, with his stress on the vital importance of baptism 'with' or 'in' the Holy Spirit. All is well: we have left the best till last! And surely this is the best part of the whole complex we know as baptism. For it is the divine part. It concerns the activity of God the Holy Spirit within the lives of the people he has sealed as his own. And it is significant that this word which signifies personal possession, 'seal' (*sphragis*), is regularly used of Christian baptism by the writers of the second century, and is linked to the Holy Spirit by the writers of the first. 'God has put his seal upon us, and given us the Spirit in our hearts as guarantee.' 'We have believed in him, and were sealed with the promised Holy Spirit' (2 Cor. 1:22; Eph. 1:14). The Book of Revelation loves to describe Christians as those who 'have the seal of God upon their foreheads' (e.g. Rev.

7:3; 9:4). Under the Old Covenant circumcision was both the sign and the seal of membership (Rom. 4:11). Under the New it is baptism; but baptism which brings us into the realm of the Spirit.

And that is just the point which the Pentecostal wants to make. Much Christian baptism does not seem to bring anyone into the realm of the Spirit. You cannot see any difference in their lives. When the Spirit came upon the Samaritans, people were left in no doubt about it. When he came upon Cornelius, everybody could see. When he came on the Day of Pentecost, it was perfectly obvious to every-body within range (Acts 8:17, 18; 10:44, 45; 2:1–13). But where is the evidence of that baptism today? It is a very old problem. John the Hermit was complaining about it in the deserts of fifth-century Syria: 'What profit have children from baptism?'

What profit indeed? And so in Pentecostal circles, and frequently in the circles of charismatic Christians, who share much Pentecostal theology, but remain in the main-line denominations, baptism in water is seen as rather unimportant, while baptism in or with the Holy Spirit is seen as crucial.

A second experience?

What do charismatic Christians mean by talk of baptism in the Holy Spirit? Naturally there are minor differences in this most dynamic movement which is all around us in the churches today, and to which I want to acknowledge my personal debt. But the main point is clear enough. Baptism with the Holy Spirit is seen as a profound and datable experience in which the Holy Spirit floods the life of the believer: it is likely to be subsequent to baptism and conversion. 'Every one needs to see that conversion and baptism in the Holy Spirit are not only separate experiences

– they are given for separate and distinct purposes. Conversion is that experience of Jesus Christ by which the non-Christian becomes a Christian, while the baptism in the Holy Spirit is that experience for the Christian to make him a powerful Christian. It is as simple as that.' (Don Basham, *Ministering the Baptism in the Holy Spirit*, p. 26f.)

Well, it would be lovely if it were as simple as that! Basham takes five passages in the Acts to justify this 'second-experience' claim. They are Acts 2:1–21, where disciples, who had long known Jesus, now experience the powerful invasion of his Spirit; Acts 8:1–17, where Samaritans had been baptised, but the Holy Spirit had not fallen on any of them before apostles came down from Jerusalem to lay hands on them; Acts 9:1–19, where we are told that there was a three-day delay between Saul's conversion and his being filled with the Spirit; Acts 10:34–46, where Basham postulates a gap of a few minutes after conversion before Cornelius and his household were baptised with the Spirit; and Acts 19:1–8 where a dozen disciples of John the Baptist on being asked, 'Did you receive the Holy Spirit when you believed?' replied, 'No, we have not even heard that there is a Holy Spirit.'

What says the Scripture?

Those passages are quite commonly adduced to justify the doctrine of a second experience, a 'baptism in the Holy Spirit' for Christians. But will they bear the weight put upon them? I doubt it. Let us glance at them in turn. Certainly the disciples had known Jesus for years and were not baptised with the Holy Spirit until Pentecost. But that is just the point! The Holy Spirit was not available to come and indwell believers until Jesus was glorified, his work of redemption done, his victory won. 'The Spirit had not been given,' remarked John in his Gospel, 'because Jesus was not yet glorified' (John 7:39). It was no 'second taste' for the disciples at Pentecost. It was very much a first taste.

It was just the same with Paul and with Cornelius. The repentance, faith, baptism and receiving of the Spirit all came within a very short time and were manifestly elements in the same process of initiation.

The only ones that look at first sight like a second experience are the cases of the Samaritans and the Ephesian dozen. The latter were clearly nothing of the kind. They had not received Christian baptism at all, we are told: only John's repentance baptism which was certainly not the same thing. Of course they did not 'receive the Holy Spirit when they believed': they did not even know that the age of the Spirit, foretold by John, had actually arrived. So they received Christian baptism and were at once plunged into the dynamic realm of the Holy Spirit. Very much a one-stage initiation.

Delay at Samaria?

We are left with only one passage about which there can be any serious doubt. Samaria. Why was there a delay between the belief and baptism of the Samaritans, and their reception of the Holy Spirit when the apostles came down from Jerusalem? Many answers have been given to this question. On any showing it is an exceptional occurrence, and it would be unwise to build a whole theology upon an exception! It is a precarious basis for Pentecostals to erect a doctrine of second blessing through the Holy Spirit, or for Catholics to build a doctrine of receiving the Spirit through episcopal confirmation. Both use this same text. They can't both be right. Is it not much more likely that neither is right? Remember, this is the first time that the gospel had been preached outside Jewish territory. Jews and

Samaritans were bitter enemies, and had been for centuries. Does this not give us a clue as to why God withheld the Spirit until Peter and John came? It was so that all could see that God received into his kingdom not only Jews but the hated and despised Samaritans too, and to reconcile these irreconcilables in Christ.

And that is why, I believe, there was such special divine overruling in the case of Cornelius. Here was the first Gentile coming to Christ. Gentiles were even more hated and despised than the Samaritans. How could God persuade his apostles, given all the prejudices of their background, to evangelise Gentiles (even though he had told them to in the Great Commission!)? Well, it took some doing. It took a vision to Peter and a vision to Cornelius to bring about their meeting in the first place! And then God stepped in and poured out his Holy Spirit upon Cornelius and friends before Peter had even finished his evangelistic sermon! God was making it plain that he accepted Gentile outsiders just as he accepted Samaritan outsiders. He has no favourites. Peter and his company got the message. 'And the believers from among the circumcised who came with Peter were amazed, because the gift of the Holy Spirit had been poured out even on the Gentiles. For they heard them speaking in tongues and extolling God. Then Peter declared, "Can any one forbid water for baptising these people who have received the Holy Spirit just as we have?"' (Acts 10:45–7.) And of course, nobody could.

So on closer inspection all five of the pillar passages usually adduced to justify the Pentecostal claim of a two-stage initiation prove insufficient to bear the exegetical weight placed upon them. Only one, the Samaritan, has any credibility at all, and for that, as we have seen, there is probably a better explanation.

'Spirit baptism'; the New Testament references

Let's come at it another way. What, according to the New Testament, is baptism 'in' (or 'by' – there is only one Greek word for both) the Holy Spirit? There are in fact seven references to it: no more and no less. And six of them refer to the contrast between the baptism of repentance which John practised, and the baptism with the Holy Spirit which his successor would inaugurate. That is the plain meaning of Mark 1:8, its parallels in Luke 3:16 and Matthew 3:11 and the near parallel in John 1:33. All make the sharp contrast between John's preparatory baptism of repentance and the baptism with the Holy Spirit which Jesus would bring.

In Acts 1:5 there is the same allusion and the same contrast. 'Wait', Jesus told them, 'for the promise of the Father, which . . . you heard from me, for John baptised with water, but before many days you shall be baptised with the Holy Spirit.' And of course it happened. Not many days afterwards, at the feast of Pentecost, when the Jews gathered to celebrate the giving of the Law to Moses, God gave his Spirit, the inner lawgiver for all believers in his Messiah to receive. He would provide not only the law of God written on their hearts, as the prophets had promised (Ezek. 36:25–32; Jer. 31:31–34; Joel 2:28f), but pardon for past failure and power for future discipleship.

The sixth reference is in Acts 11:15–16, and again it contrasts John's baptism of repentance and Jesus's baptism with the Spirit. 'As I began to speak, the Holy Spirit fell on them [i.e. Cornelius and his household] just as on us at the beginning. And I remembered the word of the Lord, how he said "John baptized with water, but you shall be baptized with the Holy Spirit."' This is one of the high points in Acts, where the Spirit of God breaks through human apartheid. That is why it is recorded no less than three

times. That is why Peter recognises it as the Gentile equivalent of Pentecost. Jesus has baptised not only Jews but
Samaritans and Gentiles with the Spirit promised long ago
by John! There are to be no distinctions between those who
have repented (11:18), believed in the Lord Jesus (11:17),
and been baptised with his Holy Spirit. One-stage initiation
throughout.

The same is true of the last New Testament reference to
'baptism in the Holy Spirit'. It comes in 1 Corinthians
12:13, 'by one Spirit we were all baptised into one body –
Jews or Greeks, slaves or free – and were all made to drink
of one Spirit.' Paul could hardly put it more plainly. Nor,
indeed, more polemically. For many of his Corinthian
readers prided themselves on remarkable gifts like
tongues, healing, prophecy, faith and so forth, and despised others. How they would have loved to claim that
only the tongues speakers, only those endowed with out-
standing gifts, were baptised in the Holy Spirit. But Paul
will have none of it. It is the one Spirit who enables people
to make the most basic baptismal confession, 'Jesus is Lord'
(12:3). And it is this one Spirit who baptises them all into
Christ, whatever the differences between them (12:13).

Only one baptism

So all seven references to 'baptism in the Holy Spirit' in the
New Testament point not to a second experience, but to an
unrepeatable, if complex, plunging into Christ, with repentance and faith, justification and forgiveness, sonship
and public witness, the gift of the Holy Spirit and the seal of
belonging, all being part of initiation into Christ. Some
parts of the whole are seen sooner than others. They may
come in different orders in different people. Some folk
seem to be very weak on repentance till long after their
conversion. Some seem to have baptism but no faith, as yet.

Some seem to have had it all for years at a low level, and then spring alive to a new dimension in the power of the Holy Spirit. But it all belongs together in the purposes of God. These are all different and complementary strands in the one and only rite of Christian initiation, baptism.

Yes, it all belongs together, even though we may experience different strands of it at different times in our lives. A person may be baptised in infancy, be converted as a teenager, and be set free to enjoy his inheritance in the Spirit years later. But they all belong together. They are all part of what makes a man a Christian, as we saw in an earlier chapter. From the point of view of the church, baptism is what does it. From the point of view of the individual's response, his repentance and faith are the crucial things. From God's point of view, what matters is his receiving of the Holy Spirit, who seals him as a member of God's family. But they are all strands in a single rope which binds a Christian to his Lord.

'Grace sometimes precedes the sacrament, sometimes follows it, and sometimes does not even follow.' So wrote Theodoret, back in the fifth century. It is perfectly obvious that vast numbers of people who have been baptised show no signs of the new life. Paul reminded the Corinthians of that danger: it had happened to their Israelite forefathers. They had all received the Old Testament prototypes of the sacraments. They had gone through the 'baptismal' waters of the Red Sea. They had been fed by the spiritual food of manna in the desert. And yet they perished in the wilderness. They had no spiritual life. And Paul reminds his readers, 'Now these things happened to them as a warning, but they were written down for our instruction . . . Therefore let anyone who thinks he stands take heed lest he fall' (1 Cor. 10:11, 12). To have received baptism and the eucharist was no more a guarantee of spiritual life or eternal security for the Corinthians – or for us – than crossing the Red Sea and eating the manna was for the

Israelites. External formalities alone never saved anyone, and it is no use relying on our baptism if we have never repented and put our faith in Christ, or received his Holy Spirit. These things jointly belong together in Christian initiation. A man is not fully a Christian until he has all three; baptism, repentance and faith, and the gift of the Holy Spirit. He may well, somewhere along the way, receive the gift of tongues along with other marks of the Spirit's presence. That is fine. But let us not call it baptism. The New Testament does not, and we shall only spread confusion if we do.

'Release' in the Spirit

What then shall we call this release to a new dimension of Christian experience and fresh spiritual gifts which many call 'baptism in the Holy Spirit'? Maybe 'release' in the Spirit is a good term. What happens, of course, is that we discover in actual experience what had been there potentially all the time in our baptism. It is a case of *possessing our possessions*. I like the story of the old lady in the Australian gold rush who was disappointed in her search, and settled down in a simple house on a little plot of land. Years later, a vein of gold was found under her house, and she mined it and became a rich woman. She had possessed that gold all along, but she was unaware that she was heir to such riches. Later on she came to enjoy what she had had a title to all the time. It is like that with the Holy Spirit. For years we may go on in our Christian life with little experience of his gifts and little expectancy of his power. And then, through God's goodness, we suddenly wake up to what we have been missing, and we claim in experience that part of our baptismal heritage in Christ which had hitherto lain largely unnoticed and unused. This may or may not be accompanied by the gift of tongues. The early Pentecostals held that this gift was the primary evidence for baptism in the Spirit. However there is little in the New Testament to back that claim, and a great many Pentecostal pastors, not to mention members, do not have the gift of tongues. As Paul puts it, 'Do all possess gifts of healing? Do all speak with tongues? Do all interpret?' (1 Cor. 12:30). Clearly not. None of us is intended by God to have all his gifts. We *are* intended to be interdependent under him, like a body under its head. And it is his responsibility to distribute spiritual gifts to the members of his body. 'The Spirit apportions these gifts' to each one individually as he wills, and it is not for our personal gratification but 'for the common good' (12:7).

Possessing your possessions

Baptism is rather like the title to a property. It is yours, in the intention of the donor, yours in all its potential, the moment you possess the title. But you may never even go to visit that property. There are lots of people who do that with the salvation to which God has offered them the title in baptism. On the other hand, you may wait for some years before you take up residence. That is your loss, but the property is still yours for the possessing, if only you will. Many people make long delay before possessing the salvation their baptism makes over to them. It is years, maybe, before they fulfil the twin conditions for actually acquiring the property, and come in repentance and faith to the Lord.

Even when you take up residence, you may live in only a few rooms of the big house, and wonder why it does not seem as good as it was cracked up to be. And then one day you come across a marvellous room, full of beautiful tapestries and costly furniture, and you wonder why you have never discovered it before. It was there all the time, of course. It was part of the inheritance to which you have the title. But you were blind to it: you had never entered in.

That is what happens when people suddenly discover a new dimension to their Christian lives, and label it 'baptism with the Holy Spirit'. It may be a misnomer, but what a glorious experience! And how we all need it. The Christian country-side is strewn with paupers who have, tucked into their pockets, the title deeds to full possession of the most marvellous mansion. But, for the most part, they have failed to realise this, or forgotten it. Some are totally ignorant, even careless, about the property. Some have begun to camp in a few of the rooms. Some have discovered and begun to enjoy the main reception rooms. But all need to be pressing on to explore and enjoy the house to the full.

'Remembering' the dying and rising life

And that is where 'remembering' comes in again. We need to remember that God has blessed us with all spiritual blessings in Christ, and that he has chosen us as his children through Jesus Christ before the foundation of the world (Eph. 1:3–4). Baptism is the seal on that election, on those blessings. All blessings we shall ever need are wrapped up in Christ. There are no blessings outside of him. And in baptism we receive the seal of incorporation into Christ. We may have repented and believed before our baptism or after: no matter. If we never repent and believe, we cannot, of course, receive any of the blessings in Christ that God has ready for us. But when we receive an overwhelming experience of the Spirit or a particular gift from his hand, it is one of the opportunities which will recur throughout our lives to 'remember', to make present in our experience here and now, the blessings that are potentially there in Christ, waiting for us to claim. So I want not just a second blessing, but a-hundred-and-second. I want to press on to know the Lord better and better – to 'know him and the power of his resurrection . . . becoming like him in his death'. That was

Paul's goal (Phil. 3:10) and it lay implicit in his baptism. For that growing entry into the dying and rising life of Jesus is nothing other than appropriating increasingly our baptismal calling. Baptism is a once-for-all experience. Unravelling its significance takes a whole lifetime. The Holy Spirit's work is potentially there in us all the time, but he waits with divine courtesy for us to recognise him, welcome him and co-operate with him. Only thus can the seed flower. Only thus can the potential become actual.

There will be times when the glory of it all will break out into singing, joy, dancing in the aisles, creative arts and special ministries. There will be other times when the gifts will seem to be taken away, and our faith will be sorely tried in some experience of spiritual wilderness. But this, too, is the work of the Holy Spirit. The cycle of death and resurrection is constantly repeated in our lives. Maybe sometimes the charismatic movement has forgotten that the Holy Spirit is at work as much in the dying as in the rising; that baptism in the Spirit will mean drowning in sorrow as well as rising up in joy; and that the Spirit of Jesus leads us to Gethsemane and Calvary as well as to Pentecost. The Spirit who came upon Jesus with such assurance and joy at his baptism is the same Spirit who led him out forthwith into the wilderness. We shall inevitably have the same variety of experience. If we think of some specially powerful and exultant times as 'a second baptism' or 'baptism with the Spirit', we shall often be desolate and wonder why that joy and exultation have gone. There will be no satisfactory answer. But if we see the highs and the lows of our experience as the outworkings of the one baptism, while the Spirit of Jesus works out in our lives the dying and the rising of the Lord, then it does become explicable. In this life, this 'vale of soul-making', he is at work on us, fashioning us by experiences of death and resurrection into his own likeness, to spend eternity with him. To be sure, the periods of darkness can be both painful and bewildering.

We may sometimes experience the Spirit's work as darkness, but we must remember that to him the darkness and the light are both alike. The dying and the rising are one work: just two different facets of it.

Unpacking God's gift

I would like to end by returning to the long letter I received from the Anglican nun I mentioned above, Sister Margaret Magdalen. She told me how, in years gone by, it was customary in religious communities to speak of taking life-long vows as 'The Second Baptism'. Now that name has been dropped, because it has been seen to be doctrinally unsound. It would be helpful if other Christians dropped it, too. For there is only one baptism, but many aspects to the heritage it offers us. Sister Margaret told me how for years she had been longing for the experience of which she had heard so much, and which many called 'baptism in the Spirit'.

> For a long time I had prayed for baptism in the Spirit, and felt puzzled and grieved that God did not appear to respond to this prayer. Then, when I became an Anglican, I was confirmed. The only sense I could make of confirmation at that stage in my life, when I had been a committed Christian and indeed a missionary for many years, was to see it as part of, and all of a piece with my baptism (which had been as a believer by immersion).
>
> So I prepared for confirmation as a deepening of the initial baptism, laying hold of the grace within that sacrament with firm hands. As the confirmation service proceeded, I became full of a radiant joy which simply overflowed – I couldn't contain it. I didn't sleep a wink that night because I was filled with praise and joy which

sometimes poured forth in tongues and sometimes took me in to a deep contemplative silence.

Next day my students [she was teaching at the time in a college of education] were awed when I began to teach them. When I asked them why they were so subdued, they told me they were afraid of the shining of my face. Like Moses I did not know that I shone.

For me, that was a mighty experience (there have been others since) of the Holy Spirit, but it was part of baptism and confirmation – all one sacrament. I realised then that I had been praying with wrong expectations before. God had now answered in *his* way.

I came to see that different baptisms, infant or adult, water or Spirit, are not necessary. One baptism is enough, and more than enough for any human being if we enter into it fully – or as fully as we can this side of the grave. We shall never fully understand the mystery of God's action for us, no matter how saintly or mature we may become. We have been given something so profound in baptism that we shall never exhaust its riches.

We have indeed. There is only one Lord. There is only one faith. And there is only one baptism, though that baptism is a many-splendoured thing. As Christians we are called to live out the dying and rising life of that one baptism in the power of the Spirit who has grafted us into the body of Christ, the one holy, catholic and apostolic church of God.